Common Sense for Uncommon Times

Common Sense for Uncommon Times

The Power of Balance in Work, Family, and Personal Life

Mark S. Guterman

Davies-Black Publishing
Palo Alto, California

Published by Davies-Black, a division of Consulting Psychologists Press, Inc., 3803 E. Bayshore Road, Palo Alto, CA 94303. 1-800-624-1765.

Cover illustration ©1994 by Liz Pichon / The Image Bank

98 97 96 95   10 9 8 7 6 5 4 3 2
Printed in the United States of America

Library of Congress Cataloging-in-Publication Data
Guterman, Mark
    Common sense for uncommon times : the power of balance in work,
    family, and personal life / Mark Guterman. -- 1st ed.
        p.   cm.
    Includes bibliographical references and index.
    ISBN 0-89106-065-0 :
    1. Conduct of life.   2. Work and family.   3. Stress management.
    4. Stress (Psychology).   I. Title
    BF637.C5G88   1994
    158 ' .1--dc20   93-41373
                    14.95   CIP

First edition
    First printing 1994

This book is dedicated to the memory of my father,

MONTY ABRAHAM GUTERMAN

Contents

CONTENTS

Preface

E arly in the process of writing this book, I was talking with a colleague who consults with organizations undergoing large, often profound change. As she described the complexities of guiding these organizations through restructuring, cultural change, team building, and other changes, she came to a sudden stop and remarked, "Almost all of what I advise these organizations and their leaders about is nothing more than common sense! Isn't it amazing how much of it they seem to have forgotten?" As I pondered what she had said, I realized that she had captured for me the heart of what so many individuals, families, and workplaces face today.

That many of us in our work, family, and personal lives have simply stopped using common sense will come as no surprise to most readers. Given the rapid pace of change, as well as the nature of the changes themselves, it is clear that these are indeed uncommon times. So uncommon, in fact, that a strong case can be made that we are in the midst of a *paradigm shift*, a postindustrial revolution that is altering how we see the world and our place in it. And whether there is agreement on what to call this age we are living through or what are its causes or ultimate outcomes, these clearly are difficult, stressful, and uncertain times.

We need only look around our own neighborhoods and workplaces to see just how stressful our lives have become. From having to do too much and making so many choices in a given day, to the uncertainty that one's job and even entire career might vanish at any instant, to the blurring of roles and relationships between men and women, to the anxiety we feel for the safety of our children and loved ones, we most definitely find ourselves crossing new and uncharted territory. In talking with thousands of people over the past several years, I've found that many feel out of control, anxious, and often unsure about the future. Similarly, many of the several dozen organizations I have worked with are behaving erratically, often making shortsighted and poor decisions as they react to the same kinds of stresses that we all face.

We not only need to reclaim our common sense, but we also must express it in a language that gives us the tools and ways for responding effectively to the new world in which we find ourselves. If we continue to react defensively and fearfully, as we seem to be doing with more frequency, we will find ourselves less able to compete and live well in a fast-moving world. I see on the horizon only more change and more stress, and those who are waiting for things to settle down or return to easier times, sadly, may find themselves increasingly unable to cope with all that awaits them. Very simply, what we need are models and methods that integrate our common sense and wisdom from the past with the realities of these uncommon times. These models, in turn, can act as guiding metaphors to help us move boldly and confidently into the new millennium.

This book has been written to introduce and describe one such model, called *generative balancing*, which is the will and capacity for creating success, finding meaning, and renewing ourselves daily and over the long haul. Generative balancing is a process whereby we can begin to build effective workplaces and well-being into our personal and family lives. It is a simple and accessible way to reclaim our common sense for the realities and needs of the twenty-first century.

In my work with individuals and organizations, I am constantly hearing the word *balance*, both in terms of how important it is and just how difficult it is to live and work this way. Given the realities of downsizing organizations and mounting work loads, there is a growing recognition that too much of our time and energy is devoted to work and not enough is left for family, play, relationships, or ourselves. Confronting this dilemma, and any number of others that we face in the years ahead, is what generative balancing and this book are all about. Whatever the daily grind—for example, getting the children dressed, fed, and to school on time, only to then face the same demands at work—many people feel out of balance, and in many ways, both obvious and subtle, they know there are better ways to work and live. Generative balancing serves both to remind us what we know and need to remember and to guide us in bringing balance to our work, family, and personal lives.

I have written this book for several reasons. The first is that without balance in our lives and workplaces, much of the joy, beauty, and grandeur of life is missing. If most of our days and nights are focused on doing and achieving, we have very little time and energy left to appreciate our accomplishments, nor do we leave any room for spontaneity, serendipity, or simply being. If we spend our so-called free time playing hard or trying to perfect ourselves and our relationships, we may get so caught up in our striving and ambition that we completely miss the experience of being alive. Generative balancing shows us how doing and being are both integral components of a healthy, productive life.

The second reason for writing this book emerges from my work with organizations. The gap between the stated company mission and the day-to-day experiences of most employees, even in many excellent organizations, is often a monumental chasm, one that profoundly impacts the long-range future of those organizations. Regardless of the reasons for this imbalance, most organizations realize they must engage the hearts, minds, and hands of all their employees if they are to achieve their goals. Generative balancing can provide the basis for a new psychological contract in which there is a direct and explicit connection between the well-being of an organization's employees and its effectiveness.

Third, and perhaps most important, I have written this book out of a desire to reach out into the future by influencing how we think and act now. I believe we have a responsibility to make the world a better, safer, and healthier place for our children, and I believe that if we lived our lives cognizant of this obligation, we would learn to behave as if the future of all of us rested with each one of us. I believe strongly that with generative balancing as a guide, we will begin living and working with greater consideration for the well-being of our children and future generations.

During a recent presentation on the balancing organization, I was asked by a retired chief executive if I had any proof or evidence that generative balancing or its methods would ensure success. "No," I responded, "I have no such proof, but if I were a betting person, I would stake everything I have on the idea that if generative balancing were built into the mission, culture, infrastructure, and human resource practices, that over time you would have a very successful organization that is both a great place to work and a model citizen in the place where it does business." He then said to me, with some skeptisism, "It's more a matter of faith, then isn't it?"—to which I heartily agreed.

And therein lies the crux of the matter. Generative balancing is as much an idea, a concept, a way of looking at and thinking about how we live and work as it is a set of methods and techniques that can easily or quickly be put to the test. It remains to be seen how generative balancing will play out in our lives and workplaces, but if we are to reclaim our common sense and eventually build a better and stronger society, I believe generative balancing is one of the ways we can begin to make this happen. I am well aware of the countervailing pressures in work, family, and personal lives, yet I do have faith that as we begin to practice and live by generative balancing, we will find ourselves more productive, healthier, more creative, and happier.

Introduction

The world which is arising is still half buried in the ruins of the world
falling into decay, and in the vast confusion of all human affairs at
present, no one can know which of the old institutions and former
mores will continue to hold up their heads and which will in the end go
under.... I see nothing at all similar to what is taking place before our
eyes. The past throws no light on the future, and the spirit of man walks
through the night.[1]

—Alexis de Tocqueville

As de Tocqueville so eloquently stated about his
time some 150 years ago, it appears that we are in
an unsettling historical period, sometimes re-
ferred to as a paradigm shift, one of monumental and profound proportions. Just as the Enlightenment and the Industrial Revolution forced
fundamental rethinking of the ways in which people lived and worked,
so, too, the present age is demanding the same. What makes this shift
different from earlier ones is also what makes it so disconcerting. Not
only are we having to adjust our minds and behaviors to accommodate
the new world, but the speed at which this is happening has even the
most capable among us reeling and confused.

Amid this radical, rapid reshaping of how we think, live, and work,
millions of people are going about their daily tasks sometimes blissfully
ignorant and at other times all too painfully aware of just what difficult

times these are. A large part of the struggle is that the stories and metaphors that guided our lives no longer work very well, if at all. In many ways, we are still thinking like a teletype machine in an age where even the lowliest home computer and facsimile machine dwarf that old and obsolete technology.

It is therefore imperative that we develop models, metaphors, and processes that accurately reflect the new and changing realities of these uncommon times, ones that are accessible to large masses of people and point us all toward the future feeling confident amid chaos, capable among uncertainty, and ready for the ambiguity and intensity that almost certainly await us. To paraphrase Albert Einstein, we can no longer solve the problems we face at the same level at which they were created. The real challenge is to create and begin to live by models that are of a different order altogether.

The model of generative balancing is one possible approach. Generative balancing is the will and capacity for creating success, finding meaning, and renewing ourselves. As the definition implies and as will be apparent throughout this book, generative balancing is much less a static state or even a goal to be achieved than it is a metaphor for living and working effectively in a world of rapid and continuous change.

Because generative balancing is a dynamic process, some of us may struggle with bringing its ideas and methods into our work, families, and personal lives. So much of our culture has for so long been built around such notions of stability, security, and control that as those have given way to instability, uncertainty, and ambiguity, we are being forced to let go of the way we used to be. The safe and simple are no longer adequate, and the degree to which we can embrace the new models and ways of doing and being is also the degree to which we can face the future with confidence and hope.

Generative balancing, as you will see throughout this book, is steeped in paradox. As we move through rapid shifts and disjointedness at home, at work, and in our relationships, we are forced to confront an increasing number of "annoying anomalies"[2] that are inherently contradictory and apparently irreconcilable. Generative balancing acknowledges that paradox is part of life and that we must learn how to live with paradoxes if we are to make our way successfully into the future. It does not try to gloss them over or deny them, but rather invites us to face them directly and then use the knowledge that we gain in this way to live and work more effectively.

Keep in mind as you read this book that generative balancing is only one way to live and work effectively in today's world. I am certain that many more working models will begin to appear, and though they all will look different on the surface, they will integrate many of the same ideas contained in this book. It is my hope that the ideas and stories you read here will inspire and assist you as you make your way into the future.

This book is neither a self-help book nor an academic treatise on the subject of balancing. Rather, it is an effort to describe the dynamic process I have called *generative balancing*. It begins by laying out the context from which the model has emerged, including how our society is imbalanced and how this stance no longer serves us well. This is followed by an overview of the model, along with details of each of its various components and characteristics. Interspersed in these chapters will be methods and techniques for creating success, finding meaning, and renewing ourselves. Suffice it to say that the model offers no multistep formulas or paths, no magical mantras or incantations, no pure research or statistical analysis of the subject. It is, instead, my own understanding of what I have seen, felt, and experienced over my lifetime, along with my efforts to communicate clearly and succinctly what I have learned.

As important as I believe the model itself is, the core of the book— its real spirit and energy—rests in the many interviews I conducted over the past year. While not all of them are detailed here, their essence is contained in those that are reported. The interviews were structured, but many of them went well beyond the initial questions.* The interviewees do not entirely mirror American society. Instead, they are

---

* See the appendix for a detailed description of the interview process and the demographics of the interviewees.

a group of articulate people who consider balance to be important in their lives and work, have given the subject some thought, and were interested enough to put their ideas and feelings into this book.

I originally intended to talk only to those who are doing the balancing "right," but as I became involved in the interviews and writing, I realized that *right* was a term that did not apply to the balancing process. I talked to people from around the country, from different professions, and of different ages and ethnic backgrounds in order to bring a sense of what people mean when they talk about balancing and the struggles and difficulties it entails. Suffice it to say at this point that the interviews were powerful, intimate, revealing, and often moving, and as you read the interviewees' stories, you will probably see much of yourself reflected in them.

These are real people, wrestling with balance not as an intellectual or philosophical exercise, but as real life, as a part of how they live and work each day. Their stories reveal the depths of their joys and pain, their frustrations and accomplishments, just how complicated it is to balance work and all the other facets of life, and how important it is for us to bring a greater sense of balance into our workplaces, families, and personal lives.

Part 1 lays out the context for generative balancing and shows the details of the model itself. It argues that we live and work in an imbalanced society and these imbalances hurt us in a world of rapid and profound change. Chapter 1 begins with the claim that balancing is innate in all living things and that we are at our best when we live and work in balance. It then cites evidence of the imbalances in our society, the reasons why we can no longer live and work this way, and how we need to live by new ways of thinking and seeing the world.

Chapter 2 introduces generative balancing and describes how it came into being. Its features and characteristics are presented, along with further reasoning about why we need new models in our lives and work. Chapter 3 introduces generative balancing's first competency, *creating success*. This is the realm in which most of us operate during our waking hours and is the dominant theme in our culture. As a society, we are fairly skilled in this competency, and this chapter proposes that there are some new ways to be thinking about achievement and accomplishment. Chapter 4 introduces the second competency, *finding meaning*, which, in contrast to creating success, is not highly valued or well developed in our culture. The competency of finding meaning and its characteristics are described fully. Chapter 5 focuses on the heart of the model, the competency of *renewal*. Providing the fulcrum or energy source for creating success and finding meaning, renewal is perhaps the toughest challenge we face on the verge of the twenty-first century. Its characteristics are laid out fully here. For each of the three competency chapters, there are charts of methods and techniques that can be learned and practiced. These are very brief so that you will be encouraged to use them as springboards to create and develop your own ways to meet your specific needs.

As a bridge between parts 1 and 2, there is a short time-out, an interlude that gives you the opportunity to reflect on what you have read and prepare you for the next section. It is an experiential exercise, guided by a set of open-ended questions that show you how to slow down and internalize what you are reading and learning in this book.

Part 2 is based on the interviews I conducted over the past year and focuses on balancing in the daily lives of individuals, couples and families, and in our workplaces. Each of the interviews is its own story and is described in the context of generative balancing. Chapter 6 shares the stories of individuals, describing their struggles and challenges, and how they see their lives as a balancing process. Chapter 7 focuses on couples and families. It shares their stories and shows their stresses and coping strategies. Chapter 8 emphasizes balancing in our organizations and workplaces, and also includes a number of workplace anecdotes and stories. In this chapter, people at the highest levels of organizations, along with a number of others, explore the challenges they face in creating and maintaining effective workplaces. At the end of each of the chapters in part 2 are summary charts describing the challenges faced by each of these groups and offering strategies for working through those challenges.

Following part 2 is a second time-out, providing another and different opportunity to experience the process of balancing. Part 3 brings the book to a close by pointing the way toward a balancing future. Chapter 9 reports on interviews with a number of balancing facilitators such as therapists, organization development specialists, and career counselors. This chapter also ends with summary charts detailing issues and challenges for this group, along with strategies for working through those challenges. Chapter 10, the conclusion, shows where we might be headed as we begin bringing generative balancing into our work, families, and personal lives.

It is my intention that this book act as personal dialogue and engagement between you and me. I hope that the writing, the concepts, the stories, and the methods and strategies not only hold your attention but also touch and move you. One thing to keep in mind is that my words and the words of all the others in this book are not meant to be taken as the one true point of view. Generative balancing is a metaphor, a way of thinking about doing and being, a guide for living and working productively, successfully, meaningfully, and fully. For many of you, it may simply be one of many guiding metaphors in your life. I believe there is much to learn from generative balancing, yet I also understand that in learning how to live effectively in the world, we all must find our own way.

PART

1

Generative Balancing

Perhaps life is not a race whose only goal is being foremost.
Perhaps true felicity does not lie in continually outgoing the
next before. Perhaps the truth lies in what most of the world
outside the modern West has always believed, namely that
there are practices of life, good in themselves, that are inherently fulfilling. Perhaps work that is intrinsically rewarding is
better for human beings than work that is only extrinsically
rewarding. Perhaps enduring commitment to those we love and
civic friendship toward our fellow citizens are preferable to
restless competition and anxious self-defense. Perhaps common
worship, in which we express our gratitude and wonder in the
face of the mystery of being itself, is the most important thing
of all. If so, we will have to change our lives and begin to
remember what we have been happier to forget.

—Robert Bellah and colleagues

Habits of the Heart

Reclaiming Our Balance

Take a couple of slow, deep breaths and recall a time in your life when you felt balanced.... How would you describe what balance looked and felt like for you? If you are like the people I interviewed for this book, many of whom you will meet in later chapters, your experience may have included a sense of calm, a feeling of lightness or peacefulness, a sense of power or of being in control, having energy, strength, or confidence, or a feeling of wholeness, of flowing, of productivity, or of being centered. When we are balanced, we are creative, productive, healthy, and satisfied. When we are out of balance, we are something less and are forced to use much of our energy, conscious or otherwise, in efforts to regain balance.

Balancing as Birthright

Balancing is our birthright and is innate in all of nature. From the macrostructures of the universe, like the galaxies and our own solar system, to the smallest subatomic particles and processes, from the interconnectedness between plants and animals, and between male and female, light and dark—balancing is a central organizing principle. It is as if balancing is hard-wired into each one of us—it is an integral part of our existence and how we live, grow, work, and play.

2   No matter where we look, what we hear, taste, touch, or feel, everything is informed by the notion of balance. That it takes both male and female to create another human being, that the earth revolves around the sun and rotates on its axis in observable and predictable ways, that our various internal systems keep us running smoothly, everything around us, everything we aspire to begins with the idea that balance is natural, necessary, and vital for existence. That we are often out of balance, individually and collectively, in no way negates the notion that balancing is our essence; whether aware of this or not, we are drawn, as a moth to a flame, in that direction. Several examples will help to illustrate.

Starting with the realm of the very small and virtually invisible, a host of exotic subatomic particles interact and interconnect with one another to create the universe we experience each day. They combine only in certain ways and are either in balance or moving toward it. Furthermore, quantum mechanics tells us that matter and energy are also interconnected and in fact are two sides of the same coin; if we try to think of them as separate and distinct, we lose the essence of both. It is also known that light has characteristics of being both a wave and a particle. Not one or the other. Not first one, then the other. Both at the same time and both always. This oneness of energy, matter, and light implies not only a delicate and profound balance but also an exquisite beauty as well.

If we look inside our bodies as another example, we see a number of elegant and sophisticated interconnected systems that define our existence, growth, and eventual death. These diverse systems are so well coordinated that we are able to achieve grace and beauty whether in movement or at rest. Guided by the principle of homeostasis, our web of systems and subsystems operates nonstop to keep us alive, as well as gives us the capacity, strength, and stability to survive and thrive on a daily basis. When we are ill, injured, or mistreated, any number of these systems work to help us regain some semblance of balance.

Balance is also at the core of virtually all religious and spiritual traditions, although there are numerous variations and ways of describing it. The Judeo-Christian idea of the Golden Rule, as well as the cycle of creation, revelation, and redemption, do not speak directly of balance, and yet a message of balance is clear. In the Chinese principles of yin and yang, a metaphor for the tension inherent in the dualities in our lives, we see that the circle is incomplete if we do not bring both sides together to form a whole. The Hindu point of view sees the physical aspect of our lives as one of only several parts of who we are, and as we come to know and experience other planes of consciousness, we then make connection with the divine. The native American tradition says that humans are part of nature, not separate from it. Ideas such as ownership and dominion over nature are anathema to native Americans and many other indigenous peoples, and instead there is intent to live in harmony, in balance, and with reverence for all that is seen and experienced.

In our environment, the surroundings in which we live, work, and play, we can observe the complex interplay of animals and plants, the myriad permutations of life, the paths and patterns of evolution. The rhythms and cycles of birth, life, and death point us to an unmistakable, albeit often brutal recognition that balance is indeed a central organizing principle in the natural world.

Finally, viewing our planet, our home, from above, as we have in pictures taken by astronauts, we have seen the earth anew and are slowly beginning to change our perspective to embrace the notion of the earth in balance. As Edgar Mitchell said during his trip to the moon:

> Suddenly from behind the rim of the moon, in long, slow-motion moments of immense majesty, there emerges a sparkling blue and white jewel, a light, delicate sky-blue sphere laced with slowly swirling veils of white, rising gradually like a small pearl in a thick sea of black mystery. It takes more than a moment to realize this is Earth...home.[3]

This reverence, so poetically described, is part of the balancing process.

The Imbalances in American Society

At the beginning of this chapter, I asked you to recall a time when you were in balance and to reexperience what that looked and felt like. If

4 you are like many of the people I know and have worked with, and like most of those I interviewed for this book, those balancing experiences are rare, happening all too long ago. Many of those I have talked with have difficulty even remembering what balancing feels like; when they do recall it, they often feel a profound loss for something missing from their lives. That so many cannot recall these times or have to go far back into their history is testament to the imbalanced lives we lead in this society.

This is not to say that for moments, or even longer, there aren't times of exquisite connection, optimal productivity, and fabulous creativity, when we and those around us are really in sync with one another. For most of us, however, these periods are the exception, not the rule. It is clear to me that American society began imbalanced and continues to be so into the 1990s. Our founding fathers and mothers, for all their wisdom and foresight, persecuted those who held contrary religious beliefs, killed indigenous peoples, owned slaves, abused and often destroyed the environment, and wrote laws and built systems to enrich and empower those who wrote the laws and built the systems. Of course, this was all done in the name of freedom and progress, from which have evolved the norms and myths that still guide us today.

There are many ways to look at our history, but however we interpret it, we cannot deny that it exerts a powerful influence on how we behave now and how we are likely to move into the future. Regardless of our individual understanding of how we got to where we are and where we go from here, I believe we find ourselves at this critical time precisely because our historical and cultural imbalance has pointed us this way. Imbalance has become so much a way of doing and being that we are hardly even aware of ourselves this way. The real difficulty is recognizing that imbalance no longer serves us well and that we need to move toward ways of thinking and behaving that are more appropriate for the demands of the twenty-first century.

A number of specific areas of imbalance will help illustrate the point. A clear example is the tendency to think only in the short term and in superficial ways about issues and problems that face us. In business, for example, many large American corporations are in trouble because they have built cultures, procedures, and processes that look only at the next several months, or the next year or two at most. Whether due to shareholder expectations, compensation plans that reward only the near term, or our own individual needs, as soon as someone begins talking about five, ten, or twenty years into the future, eyes glaze over, listening stops, and decision makers do what they have typically been rewarded for: Ignore the long-range consequences in favor of the short-term payoffs.

Similarly, as individuals, we are often attracted to quick, easy fixes for complicated, ambiguous problems. In our haste to ease our pain and struggles, most of us choose the easy, safe route over the difficult, risky paths often necessary to get to the heart of the matter. One need only look at political campaigns to realize that even at the pinnacle of leadership there is often little deep or sustained effort to engage the real issues of the day.

Furthermore, acquisition and ownership is endemic to our society, and consumerism becomes a passion for the day. We are burdened by products we do not need, supported by vast amounts of advertising designed to make us believe that these products are necessary for fulfillment and meaning.

Another example of imbalance is the emphasis on winning and winners, ignoring the often excellent efforts and hard work of other members. Anything short of finishing first is branded as failure. Watch, for example, the faces and emotions of those who finish second in any significant sporting event, and the point is clear. We often forget that all of us, all the time, are finishing second, third, or, even worse still, "out of the money." When we don't "measure up," we feel like failures.

Finally, think of the imbalance caused by our market-oriented worldview. Our cultural bias sees products, deliverables, numbers, titles, results, and doing as guiding principles. This active stance and conception of things as discrete, separate entities leads us to value results over process, power over collaboration, mastery over intimacy, networking over connecting, and competition over cooperation. This is not to imply that the former in each of these dichotomies is

6 necessarily bad. Rather, it is to say that this particular mind-set is incomplete and therefore a source of continuing imbalance.

There are certainly other examples of imbalance in our society. Specifics aside, however, the driving force behind this imbalance comes from a basic dualism, a habit of seeing, thinking, and even feeling things as either/or, seeing ourselves as winners or losers, right or wrong, conservatives or liberals, thinkers or feelers. Our tendency to dichotomize the world simplifies what we see and, up to a point in our history, has made life easier. In the world we are now entering, though, one that is filled with ambiguity, uncertainty, and profound change, this dualism is quickly becoming obsolete, and perhaps even dangerous.

Nowhere is this more cogent than in the area of diversity. As we find ourselves more and more living and working with people and ideas that are "foreign" to us, we need to be ever diligent not to fall into a "we/they" way of thinking that may prevent the understanding, compassion, or empathy needed for a positive coexistence. A tenacious clinging to "us" thinking as our society becomes more diverse promises to be a great source of difficulty in the years ahead.

To ensure progress toward resolution of the imbalance inherent in our modern life, we need to take the time and energy to understand the nature of the issues, how they are interconnected with one another and each of us, and how solutions require fundamentally new ways of thinking and acting.

Reclaiming Balance

Reclamation of balance begins by questioning basic assumptions about who we are, how we live and relate to one another, and how we shall move into the future. We need to question many of the assumptions of our culture:

- Continuous growth and progress are good.
- Those who work hard and play by the rules will be the most successful.

- That which can be seen and quantified deserves most if not all of the rewards.
- America has been chosen to bring democracy, freedom, and capitalism to a world that is eager to embrace what we have.
- Competition is always good.

Because many of these assumptions may no longer be valid in the world in which we live, continued acceptance will be a source of much pain and difficulty.

Rigorous and continuous questioning of basic social and cultural assumptions will be a major tenet of any new models that will guide us into the future. Even the principles upon which the models are built will be open to question. Therefore, one of the ways we will move toward balance will be to recognize that our new models are not static, but changing and dynamic, reflecting and describing the world in increasingly accurate, deep, and subtle ways. They will help us to appreciate that our work and lives, as well as the environment, represent not simply problems to be solved or answers to be found, but rather are always in the process of growing, developing, and moving toward balance.

The new models that will show us how to reclaim balance will also be accessible to ever-increasing numbers of people and will require less from experts and gatekeepers. The language will be simple and straightforward and will work for individuals, families, and organizations; the core concepts will be the same for all. The methods rising from the new models will by design and necessity come from the day-to-day needs of real people, families, and workplaces as they find their way toward an increasingly uncertain future.

Furthermore, we can only reclaim balance if our new models are integrated and comprehensive and more holistic. Rather than having to rely on different sources for the various aspects of one's work and life, the new models will act as central organizing principles that may work, with adaptation and modifications, over a lifetime and more. This means that the good models will begin to approach in the social sphere what physicists are now trying to discover, the so-called *theory of*

8 *everything!* As we develop our understanding in this way, we will be able to see and explain the big picture, the current issue or question, as well as how the two are interconnected. Achieving a centered and purposeful life will become a reality for most people.

Generative balancing is one of these new models built from the foundation just described and designed to show us how to reclaim balance in our work and lives. As this model is described in the next four chapters, keep in mind that I offer it not as a be-all or end-all, but rather as a new "story," most of which is still waiting to be told. Some of that story you will hear in later chapters from the people I interviewed for this book. The rest is yours to create. As you read, ponder, and assimilate the words here, I hope you will find the inspiration and motivation to write and enact your own story of balancing.

2

The Generative Balancing Model

Balancing is not only our birthright; it is the key to well-being, productivity, health, and even happiness. Those readers who have experienced times of balance know how powerful they are and that it makes sense, given the challenges we face in the coming years, to develop, internalize, and use a model that is built from the notion of balance.

Generative Balancing Defined

The model for generative balancing is shown in figure 1, which illustrates the three parts, or competencies, that comprise the model: creating success, finding meaning, and renewal. As anyone who has ever been on a seesaw knows, if there is too much weight on one side, we end up either on the ground or suspended helplessly in the air, and invariably all the fun of the ride is gone. As described earlier, we have put too much weight on creating success, and in this way the seesaw does not work well. Further, if the weight is unevenly distributed, we find ourselves having to expend excess energy just to keep moving, and again are less able to enjoy the fun of the ride. The fulcrum, renewal, is

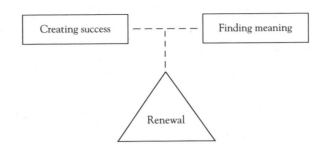

Figure 1   Generative Balancing

the point of connection for the three parts of the model and provides all the energy. All three elements are necessary for balancing, and the real thrill, the excitement of the ride—just as in life—comes from the movement, not from finding a steady-state point of balance in the middle, which is why the word *balancing* is emphasized in this book.

Earlier I described how generative balancing implies the will and capacity for creating success, finding meaning, and renewing ourselves. Before discussing the three parts of the model, it is important to understand what is meant by will and capacity. *Will* is both the readiness and motivation to engage each of the elements of the model; *capacity* represents the discipline and tools necessary to make each part of the model real and manifest in one's life—on the seesaw, this means having the strength to climb on, get it going, and keep it moving. Without both the will and capacity, balancing is not achievable.

Implicit in the definition is also the will and capacity to move fluidly and adeptly across any or all parts of the model. This means that there will be times when we will devote more time and energy to creating success than finding meaning, and other times when we will jump off to repair the fulcrum or just take a time out from the ride altogether. Being aware of the whole model, knowing that there is more to it than the part we are focusing on at the moment is perhaps the most challenging part of moving toward balance in our work and lives.

Creating success, which will be discussed in more detail in chapter 3, revolves around accomplishment and achievement and is the "doing" aspect of the model. Not only is this the most visible part of the model, but for many of us it is the one and only game in town. It has three components: discovering, visioning, and navigating. Creating success, as the most observable and tangible competency of generative balancing, can in some ways be thought of as the body of the model. Though creating success is essential for balancing, our cultural overemphasis on this competency rarely is enough to give us a true and deep sense of ease and well-being.

Finding meaning, to be discussed in chapter 4, has to do with purpose in our work and lives and is the "being" aspect of the model. Meaning is much less visible and obvious than success and can be thought of as the mind of the model, or something akin to an individual's identity or an organization's culture. It also has three components: being, connecting, and acting. As the diagram for the model indicates, it can be thought of as the counterpoint to creating success; without meaning, it is impossible to move toward balance in our work, family, and personal lives.

Renewal, the subject of chapter 5, is the heart of generative balancing, both because of its own importance and because it lends life and energy to success and meaning. Renewal is seeing and experiencing each day and each moment as new—as if each day were the only one there is. Renewal is the least visible part of the model; as the energy behind what we do and who we are, renewal can be likened to the spirit of the model.

All three parts of the model must be present in order to begin moving toward balance. Yet the model of generative balancing, no matter how it is depicted, is only a metaphor to help guide us toward balance in our work and lives. The picture, the model, and even the words for it are most of all suggestive for how we might move toward greater well-being, productivity, health, and happiness.

How Generative Balancing Came Into Being

When I returned to school fifteen years ago to begin working on my counseling degree, I immediately became intrigued by the various

12 models and theories that assisted people in their growth and development. Not only did each have its own language and biases, but each claimed to be a more accurate picture of the truth. There were areas of overlap, of course, but because their conceptual frameworks were often couched in esoteric, inaccessible language, it was often difficult to compare the models or theories.

Having so many ways of describing our world, with few people understanding how they were interconnected, was only made worse when the latest "new and improved" therapy or method was introduced. These best-sellers were usually only updated, often incompatible, versions of last year's model. Further, as I began to study, I found that much of what was being touted in the popular culture was either ungrounded in research or real-world experience, or was so esoteric and inaccessible that only the "experts" could communicate the knowledge. This meant that new, emerging practices were either not worth much or were subject to potential abuse by the leaders teaching and promoting them.

As a result, I began looking for common themes and underlying principles in order to build an integrated, comprehensive model of growth and development that would be both deep enough and broad enough to work for individuals, families, and organizations. My first real effort was a counseling model that brought the concepts of self-acceptance, self-actualization, and self-realization together in a single, albeit linear, model. Although my papers and presentations were often soundly criticized, I sensed that my work in reaching for a set of core concepts was on track. I also knew that the organizational piece of the puzzle was missing, and that without that, my efforts would at best be insufficient.

After receiving my degree, I worked in human resources for a large, rapidly growing retail firm. I could see almost immediately that the ways the decision makers saw the world was not only different from most employees' perceptions, but that a different language was being used to describe various needs and wants. Managers spoke of efficiency and productivity, and employees talked about growth, satisfaction, and contribution. The unifying principle was success, but the language and mechanisms for bringing the two together did not exist. I soon found through my work and by talking with colleagues in other organizations that this was a common experience and a problem of increasing urgency. Many efforts were under way to bridge the gap, most notably the much-touted quality circles, but as with similar efforts today, their impact was limited and short-lived.

Over the course of the next five years, I began building models attempting to describe the problem and to offer prescriptions for achieving both organizational effectiveness and employee well-being. My first complete version was entitled "Organization Development and Renewal: A New Model." I began presenting it in management classes and seminars every chance I got.

With each presentation and continuing study, I heard feedback, stories, and additional ideas, and so the model continued to be refined. It began informing and guiding my work and life, and was working for others as well: One person used its key concepts in the design of a teen parent program; another used it in work with the developmentally disabled; and still another used it to redesign a company-wide management training program. Once I saw its range, I was even further convinced that this was a useful and expansive model that would undergo modifications and refinements; it would be a truly generative model, a model in process.

What you are reading here, then, is, in the truest sense of the word, a work in process. It is my hope, as I said in the preface, that you will use what you read and learn here in your own work and life, and will make this just the starting place from which to bring your life and work into greater balance.

Characteristics of the Generative Balancing Model

Though still evolving, generative balancing, as a guiding metaphor or central organizing principle for our work, family, and personal lives, has been built to be both comprehensive and integrated. The competencies

14 of the model can apply to all aspects of our lives, such as in our workplaces, politics, and community growth. Its simple language has an integrating sensibility so that when we talk of responsibility, for example, these same concepts work well across the various parts of our lives. Balancing is the unifying principle of the model.

Generative balancing is both descriptive and prescriptive. It both describes what is going on in our work and lives and acts as a guide for moving into the future.

Because generative balancing reflects deeply who we are and what we aspire to become, it is naturally paradoxical in nature. If you are looking for neat, clean, smooth, or consistent, generative balancing is not for you. In fact, it will become clear that this model, much like life itself, has inconsistencies; it is designed to guide our work and lives as they are and can be, not as we wish they were or believe them to be. Forcing ourselves to confront and deal with the paradoxes in our lives may be unsettling and difficult, but it is one of our major tasks.

Finally, generative balancing, like most models, creates as many new questions as it answers. By encouraging continuous questioning as one of its key attributes, it not only forces us to challenge our assumptions, it also brings us face-to-face with what and how much we do not know. As in confronting paradox, this stance of questions begetting more questions may be unsettling for a number of readers. However, if the model is truly to serve as a guide for moving into the future, it can certainly do no less. As you read the following chapters, you may find that the suggested questions are only the beginning of a long, exciting process of growth and learning.

Why We Need a Model Like Generative Balancing and Why Now

Much of the usefulness of generative balancing lies in its ability to capture and label the issues confronting society for many individuals, families, and workplaces. It can teach individuals, families, and organizations how to cope and even thrive in these rapidly changing times. It teaches users to ask important questions throughout life, many of which are currently ignored, others difficult to ask. But it is my firm belief that the degree to which we are willing to wrestle with these questions is also the degree to which we will begin moving toward real wisdom. Explicit questions are part of the model and are a key component of learning and moving toward balance.

By focusing on the competencies of generative balancing, people can learn, internalize, and practice living and working with a greater sense of control in their lives. Because generative balancing is a lifelong practice, one that in many ways is never truly mastered, it helps people to identify what they can and cannot control, and how and when to let go, as necessary. It can point the way to living calmly and peacefully in an often chaotic world, and therefore living and working more effectively.

Organizations, too, spend an inordinate amount of resources trying to control the environment through such methods as advertising, legislative initiatives, rewards and punishments, and buying or borrowing data and people from competitors. A number of astute leaders are beginning to realize that in a global economy, the idea of control is mostly a myth. They have discovered that as they let go of their need to control their markets, people, and information, they are free to focus on core business issues and to form strategic alliances that take them beyond where they could ever go alone. Generative balancing shows organizations and leaders how to live effectively with this paradox: To those who can let go accrues true power.

Generative balancing also emphasizes the importance of connections at the very time when our sense of community is perhaps at its most fractured in our history. It is clear in my work as a counselor and consultant, as well as in what I have heard in the interviews for this book, that deep and abiding connections are crucial, yet so few people have the time and energy to form and nurture them. Generative balancing sees connecting as both important and necessary in our work and lives and shows us ways to build this into our daily activities.

16   Some organizations, too, are beginning to recognize the importance of connecting. Progressive leaders recognize that their organizations mean more to communities than the number or quality of the jobs they provide. The esprit de corps and synergy created by community-sensitive companies can be seen in school–business partnerships, support of cultural and sometimes controversial events, and grass-roots community building that a number of companies around the country are supporting. Generative balancing suggests that connecting is at the core of being a good corporate citizen and is ultimately a bottom-line issue as well.

On a more personal level, generative balancing teaches people to be aware of stress and how to manage its impact in our lives and in workplaces. By emphasizing that meaning and renewal are just as important as success, it shows people that other, less visible aspects of their lives need to be honored and supported. Organizations are also beginning to recognize that stress has a subtle and profound influence on productivity, and employee assistance programs, stress management seminars, and flextime have emerged from this awareness.

Perhaps most importantly, generative balancing shows people and organizations how to develop a larger, longer-term perspective through its emphasis on questioning and by promoting skills that only emerge after a long period of concerted effort. Eventually, those workplaces that operate by this longer-range perspective will become, I believe, more effective and most certainly better places to work. For individuals and families, this perspective helps them see into the lives of their children and descendants, helping them develop a greater sense of peacefulness, even if their daily lives are difficult and chaotic.

Generative balancing is not a panacea or quick fix, but more a beacon toward which we aspire.

3

Creating Success

T he first competency of generative balancing is our will and capacity for creating success. As a society, in our workplaces, and as individuals, we are mostly very good at this; all our accomplishments and achievements result from our competency in this realm. As you read this chapter, you may want to assess your own competence vis-à-vis the various attributes of creating success.

As figure 2 indicates, there are three components in creating success, each having a number of distinct attributes. *Discovering* is the uncovering and articulation of those characteristics that brought us to where we are now, as well as readying oneself or the workplace for using that information to move forward. *Visioning* is the process of vividly imagining and focusing clearly on a desired future state. And *navigating* is the process of moving toward our vision in a step-by-step, action-oriented fashion.

Discovering

Discovering helps us bring the past into focus through a search for such specifics as themes, patterns, strengths, weaknesses, core properties, and likes and dislikes in order to understand how we got to where we are.

Attributes	Components		
	Discovering	Visioning	Navigating
Questions	Where am I now? How did I get here? What lessons have I learned and how do I use them as I move into the future?	Where do I want to go? When do I want to get there?	What steps do I take to achieve my goals?
Attitudes and Beliefs	Readiness Curiosity Acceptance	Optimism Idealism Imagination	Risk orientation Flexibility Intentionality
Knowledge, Skills, and Abilities	Self-assessment ability Ability to reflect	Decision-making skills Goal-setting skills Information-processing skills Action-planning skills	Implementation tools Measurement and evaluation skills Feedback and course correction skills

Figure 2   Creating Success

By having this information clearly in front of us, we can make better decisions about the future. Also, the process itself of discovering, regardless of what we find out about ourselves or our workplaces, is valuable in that we learn to attribute our successes and failures to the right qualities. In short, discovering teaches us how to be honest about where we are and how we got there.

Discovering Questions

The discovering questions, though relatively straightforward and easy to ask, are often not voiced regularly by individuals, families, and organizations. The first of these—Where am I now? (plural, of course, for families and organizations)—forces us to stop doing long enough to listen for an answer. As most readers know, taking time for even this initial question is often difficult. The follow-up question—How did I get here?—helps us understand how our actions and behaviors created the results we see before us. These two questions are interlocking, and unless we ask both, we run the risk of never being quite sure of ourselves and our role in our accomplishments and achievements.

The third question—both the most important for discovering and all too infrequently asked—is, What lessons have I learned and how do I use them as I move into the future? This question requires us to be reflective and to then internalize the knowledge we gain as a result. Both parts of the question take time and honesty, and in my work with individuals and organizations, I see that this is one of the trickiest and most difficult questions I can pose. If we were to take time each day to ponder this question, however, our future might be different.

Discovering Attitudes and Beliefs

The first attitude or belief that characterizes discovering is best captured by the word *readiness*. Anyone who has ever tried to help someone or create change in an organization knows that until the readiness is there, most of our efforts are for naught. Readiness means that we are prepared to give the time, energy, and attention necessary to engage the questions just given, as well as others that inevitably emerge along the way. Being ready, however, does not necessarily imply that we have the patience or perseverance to find the answers. Readiness does recognize that fear, denial, and resistance are normal and human and are nearly always present in the process of discovering.

Another attitude or belief necessary for discovering is *curiosity*. In its simplest terms, curiosity is an openness to seeing and experiencing things as they are. This implies a suspension of judgment when gathering information and data, as well as being delighted by surprises that inevitably occur while discovering. Furthermore, embedded in curiosity is the capacity for not always having to know the answers. This last aspect—and, indeed, curiosity itself—is often in short supply for people in positions of power, whether in families, communities, workplaces, or politics.

The third, and most subtle, discovering attitude or belief is that of *acceptance*—a willingness to own all of our actual past, not as we fantasize or rationalize it to be. Many of us—individuals, families, and organizations—are continuously revising our histories in order to dampen a difficult past, downplay our roles in mistakes or failures, or simply make us feel better about who we are. Not only is acceptance one

20 of the keys to self-esteem and mental health, but until we can accept things and ourselves at face value, all of our efforts toward balancing will be fruitless.

Discovering Knowledge, Skills, and Abilities

The first skill involved with discovering—*self-assessment*—is actually a cluster of abilities that includes knowing how to clarify our values, identifying our strengths and weaknesses, knowing our likes and dislikes, and making sense of the patterns of our experiences. While this may sound simple at first, anyone who has gone through any serious career counseling knows that self-assessment can be difficult and time-consuming. Those clients who have learned this skill are not only more adept at wrestling with the discovering questions but are also able to bring them into other parts of their lives and work.

Another skill area important to discovering is the ability to *reflect*. For our purposes, reflection is the ability to look both inward and back in time, to make sense of what we see, and to learn from the experience. In our culture, reflection is not highly valued or practiced with much skill; what reflection there is often becomes a trivial pursuit of nostalgia. Real, honest reflection is essential if we are to hear and learn lessons from our past, which then can form the basis from which to create a better future for ourselves, our families, and our workplaces.

Methods and Techniques for Discovering

For Individuals

- Keep a journal and make regular entries, with particular emphasis on engaging any or all of the discovering questions.
- Work with a therapist, counselor, support group, or other helper if the discovering questions are difficult or bring up undue pain.
- Spend time clarifying values, identifying interests, and trying to articulate the guiding themes in your life, either through some previously organized program or on your own.

For Couples and Families

- Follow all the suggestions for individuals, shared with one another.
- Find time to share family stories and myths. Encourage all family members to participate and examine them thoroughly.
- Hold regular dialogues with one another that are centered on the ideas "Here is how I see and experience you" and "How do you see and experience me?"

For Groups and Organizations

- Appoint someone as an historian to chronicle the history and key events of the group or organization. This should be a trusted and honest person whose charter is to record, report, analyze, and offer commentary on the workings of the group or organization, and who reports the findings to the leaders on a regular basis. All members should also be allowed access to this information.
- Create space and time for reflection. This can include "quiet space," a "thinking room," and week-ending closure/reflection meetings that center on the ideas "What did we accomplish this week?" and "What learnings can we take into next week?"
- Initiate meetings in which leaders and other members across the organization meet regularly to wrestle with the discovering questions. The norms of these meetings can be built from the discovering attitudes and beliefs and can be facilitated by someone who is particularly competent in discovering.

Visioning

Visioning is the process of articulating as clearly as possible a desired future state. It rests on the assumption that goals that can be seen and felt have great power to move us forward. Many clients, both individuals and organizations, have spoken eloquently of the "compelling" nature of their vision, or even of being "pulled" forward by its energy and appeal. Visioning enhances our power and rivets our energy on our goal.

Visioning Questions

The visioning questions, again, are straightforward and easy to ask, but many people are unable to sustain the asking long enough to know what their vision is. The first question is, Where do I want to go? Or, What do I want my life, family, community, work, organization, business to look like at some ideal time in the future? Clearly, some can get caught up in the fantasy of the future, but for those who have persevered, somewhere during the process of asking this question a vision is revealed and made clear.

The second question provides some boundaries to the previous one: When do I want to get there? Some of my career change clients develop inspiring visions that never materialize. A major reason, I believe, is that without some sense of *when* it will happen, it is difficult to sustain the energy necessary when navigating our way to our goal. By asking ourselves when we hope to achieve it, we can heighten the motivation necessary for that achievement.

Visioning Attitudes and Beliefs

The first visioning attitude or belief is *optimism*, which is our sense of hopefulness about the future and our faith that our life and work will lead us ultimately to our goal Throughout my work and the interviews for this book, I have been continually struck by the degree of optimism in most people. In spite of current difficulties, whether in personal lives or in work, it is clear that optimism is a deep and abiding attitude in our culture.

The second attitude or belief important to visioning is *idealism*, another basic American attitude. In spite of flaws and persistent problems, most Americans remain idealistic, sometimes to the point of naïveté. Our capacity to be guided by idealism, to give ourselves permission to dream grandly, is crucial for balancing.

The third attitude or belief important to visioning is *imagination*— the willingness to free one's mind to create or sense possibilities. While imagination comes naturally and easily for young children, few adults know how to use imagination well. One could surmise that our inability to work through the chaos and complexities of modern life comes from a failure of imagination and that our health and prosperity ultimately rest on a capacity to free ourselves from past habits to see as yet unimagined possibilities.

Visioning Knowledge, Skills, and Abilities

Visioning skills are well developed in many parts of our society, and most successful people and workplaces are fairly adept in these areas. The first of these, which is critical to all the others, is decision-making ability, or how we discern, from what we see and know, the course of action most likely to take us to our destination. There are numerous techniques to help us in decision making, the most critical of which is the integration of the rational and data-driven side of the equation with our less rational and intuitive side. The best decisions of the future will most likely be those that involved rational thinking and intuition as appropriate to the decision-making processes at the time.

Goal setting is the second necessary visioning skill and refers to the application of decision-making ability to prioritize our needs and desires. Many of my clients have had great difficulty setting goals, either due to "paralysis by analysis" or because so much of what's out there looks and feels interesting. Individuals and organizations who are unable to set goals often do not live up to their potential and can usually benefit from more balance in their lives.

Another crucial skill in visioning is information processing, which is knowing where and how to get the necessary information, having the necessary critical thinking skills to sift through the information quickly and accurately, and knowing how to frame that information so that the vision continually becomes clearer. Supporting each of these steps is the skill of knowing how to use the necessary technology in appropriate ways. Further, regardless of what information we need or the methods by which we obtain it, we must also be able to make sense of it quickly without having to wait to gather all the pieces. Our capacity for rapid conceptualizing will become increasingly important in the years ahead.

The fourth skill area for visioning is actually the bridge between visioning and navigating. This is the ability to develop the strategies, plans, and steps necessary to begin actually moving toward our goals.

24 Many of us are fairly accomplished at this, but two areas in particular cause difficulty for large numbers of individuals and organizations. The first is the tendency to jump into action before thinking through the plans, resulting in workplaces where the cultural norm is "ready, fire, aim." The second is that even our well-thought-out plans often look only to the short term and often do not recognize the alternatives and contingencies that may be necessary to achieve more long-range goals.

Methods and Techniques for Visioning

For Individuals

- Articulate goals in visual and other nontraditional ways, such as drawing, painting, sculpting, model building, calligraphy, or poetry.
- Describe goals in terms of senses other than sight. For example: How does my goal make me feel? What messages do I hear from my goal? Does my goal have a taste, and if so, what is it?
- Keep a representation of your goal close to you at all times. Look at it, think about it, and add to or modify it as appropriate.

For Couples and Families

- Follow the suggestions for individuals, shared with one another.
- Create a "visioning wall" or post a large sheet of paper on which all members can write or draw their sense of the goals.
- Hold periodic meetings, explicitly focusing on the question, What is our shared vision together?
- Make time for "outrageous delusions," during which everyone can think big and be supported to express even the most outlandish ideas freely.

For Groups and Organizations

- Offer processes, mechanisms, and technology that teach members how to work toward a shared vision.

- Create strategic planning processes that allow input from all parties who have a stake in the vision, as well as engaging both the hearts and minds of all concerned.
- Build creative problem-solving expertise into the group or organization, with particular emphasis on nonrational methods such as visualization or guided imagery.

Navigating

Navigating, the third component of creating success, is composed of the steps we take toward our goals. When we observe individuals, families, and workplaces going through the tasks of the day, most often we are witnessing them navigating toward some goal. Without this movement, visions remain fantasies and wishful thinking. Embedded in navigating is also the notion that these same movements are rarely a straight shot toward the goal. Instead, moving toward the distant shore is a series of zigs and zags, lulls combined with full speed ahead. It is from disciplined action over time that we see the achievement of our goals.

Navigating Questions

There is one key question in navigating: What steps do I take to achieve my goals? Seemingly obvious, this question must be asked before each step along the way, because with each step taken comes new information that may then affect subsequent steps. In personal, family, and work lives, our plans for achieving goals must honor contingencies, recognize and respond to barriers and setbacks, and accept that the course consists of just as much side stepping, backtracking, and holding firm as it does moving directly toward the goal. The trick, once again, is the persistent movement over time, prompted by asking the key question.

Navigating Attitudes and Beliefs

The first attitude or belief of navigating is having a risk orientation, a willingness to experiment, make mistakes, and not be afraid of failing.

26 Many individuals and organizations have seen their glorious goals and plans go up in smoke simply because of risk aversion. Those who can see that all movement toward goals is essentially about the unknown recognize the pervasiveness of risk. Those most willing to risk will also gain from the mistakes they may make along the way.

Being open-minded about the risks necessary for creating success is one thing; being flexible in our plans and actions is something else altogether. Flexibility—being able to tolerate ambiguity and change course if necessary—is key to success and balancing. The difficulty for many, however, is that at the heart of flexibility is a willingness and comfort with not having all the answers. For most adults I know, especially those in positions of power, this last proposition is extremely difficult.

The third attitude or belief important to navigating is *intentionality*, which in many ways is counterpoint to flexibility. It has to do with focusing our energies and efforts on the goal, as well as having the inner drive to stay the course until it is achieved, especially through the tough times. Intentionality and flexibility, paradoxical though they may seem, are necessary together, in sufficient strength and appropriate proportions, if we are to achieve our goals and move toward balancing in our work, family, and personal lives.

Navigating Knowledge, Skills, and Abilities

Navigating begins with having the necessary and appropriate tools, whether these be the technical skills to do a task or the personal qualities to work through the task. If the individual, family, or organization does not have these tools, then at least part of the navigating process must be devoted to acquiring and learning how to use them. Further, however skilled we are at the beginning of our journey, our tools must be updated and enhanced along the way, especially if we are moving into uncharted territory.

Also important in navigating are evaluation and measurement skills. We are fairly adept at measuring things like output per hour, chores or tasks completed, miles run, or activities planned and completed.

However, to measure the qualitative side of these things, for example, how they rate in terms of effectiveness, individual well-being, effort, and consequences, is another thing altogether. In the years ahead, as we work more with our minds in assimilating information and with people and systems that have a number of real differences, our capacity to quantify, measure, and evaluate both efforts and results will become increasingly important, requiring subtle, sophisticated tools and training. These new ways of measurement and evaluation will offer areas of work and business to those individuals and organizations who can find ways to build bridges between efforts and results.

A third area important in navigating is in feedback and course correction skills. Feedback concerns both the giving and receiving of useful information. If we are unable or unwilling to discern the key messages along our path, the knowledge necessary for achieving our vision will elude us. Similarly, unless we can give feedback effectively to others, the relationships we have—as parents, partners, lovers, colleagues, co-workers, or supervisors—may get in the way of moving toward mutually desirable goals. And, of course, feedback must then be integrated into our plans so that we can change course as necessary. Part of our course-changing ability rests in our flexibility, but even more important is the recognition that prior efforts and progress, no matter how far off course we may be, should be recognized and valued for the knowledge gleaned and for the experience itself.

Methods and Techniques for Navigating

For Individuals

- Learn the skills necessary to achieve your goals, whether these be, for example, technical, functional, or interpersonal.
- Take time-outs to measure and document your progress, seek feedback, adjust your course of action, and give yourself an occasional breather.
- Build time lines that are both realistic and flexible.

- Keep résumés, portfolios, vitae, and other important documents up-to-date.
- Reward yourself for serious efforts toward your goal, even if the results were less than satisfactory.

For Couples and Families

- Follow all of the suggestions for individuals, shared with one another.
- Design and implement projects that build both individual and couple/family skills, such as community activism, coaching, and assisting children with homework.
- Share stories of success, including those in which barriers have been overcome, to motivate everyone to move forward together.

For Groups and Organizations

- Design and institute reward systems that recognize and pay for skills acquisition and mastery.
- Evaluate performance honestly and timely. The methodology or format is less important than the fact that feedback must be straightforward and truthful. Also, data from a variety of sources makes performance feedback more credible and often easier to communicate.
- Train continuously, formally and informally, in both technical/funtional skills and communication/human relations skills.
- Build quality into every step of the group or organizational process, both as a cultural norm and as the way in which you conduct business.
- Measure both the quantitative and qualitative aspects of the group or organizational process, especially those difficult-to-measure human relations practices.

In Summary

Most of us spend the better part of our waking hours in the pursuit of creating success. American culture values these efforts and actions, so substantial rewards go to those most competent in this realm. Because potential rewards are so high and so visible, we stay in jobs, for example, that are often unhealthy, or build products that are dangerous to employees and the environment, or stay with partners who abuse us. Creating success is the focus of most of our energy, but in the quest for accomplishment, we may lose sight of the balance and wisdom needed for the accomplishment.

Creating success is no longer enough for most people. Whether because we are educated differently than earlier generations or because our awareness has changed due to what we have learned or lived through in the last half century, our need and desire for achievement is now tempered by the recognized importance of such things as effort, responsibility, positive attitude, intention, and support of the learning process. Creating success in terms of observable, measurable results alone is insufficient.

In our drive to reach our goals, we need to honor our need and desire for time out, not just the couple of weeks vacation each year, but daily time and space for reflection, observing, and daydreaming. We can no longer focus only on the traditional notions of success, accomplishment, and achievement. We must pay attention to the need for meaning and renewal, needs that cannot be addressed under our current ways of working and living. If we live and operate only for success, we will find ourselves, as we have throughout history, swinging from one imbalance to another. We must honor that which is our real nature—to be in balance.

4

Finding Meaning

The second competency of generative balancing is the will and capacity for finding meaning and fulfilling our purpose, something our culture is not particularly good at. As you read this chapter, you may want to assess yourself concerning each of the characteristics of finding meaning.

As figure 3 indicates, there are three components in finding meaning, each having a number of distinct attributes. *Being* is the inner experience of an individual, family, or organization and is composed of those traits that define and establish who we are. *Connecting* is a coming together and interacting in a meaningful fashion, often to accomplish, often simply to be together. *Acting*, which builds on and deepens navigating, emphasizes movement both toward our goals and our purpose. The remainder of the chapter will describe each component in detail.

Being

Being is our essence. It is those qualities and traits that distinguish who we are. From an individual perspective, this is best described by the words *identity* or *personality*. From a workplace point of view, it would

32

Attributes	Components		
	Being	Connecting	Acting
Questions	Who am I? What is my purpose?	How do I create and nurture the relationships necessary for my vision and purpose?	How do I achieve my vision and purpose? How do I achieve success and at the same time experience a sense of meaning and fulfillment?
Attitudes and Beliefs	Integrity Appreciation Presence	Cooperation Compassion Trust Differences valued	Responsibility Courage Patience Perseverance
Knowledge, Skills, and Abilities	Ability to clarify values, identify needs and wants Ability to accept fears, defenses, and barriers	Communication skills Group process and conflict resolution skills Linking ability	Follow-through ability Ability to focus and concentrate Ability to work through fears, defenses, and barriers

Figure 3   Finding Meaning

be the *norms, myths,* and *values* that comprise the workplace culture. From either side, these elements are much less visible than our outward appearance or our actions, and often we do not know or understand our own essence. Slowing down long enough to know and experience who we are is extremely difficult in modern life. Yet virtually everyone I spoke with and thousands of others I have met with in my work have said in so many words that being is one of the keys to balancing our work, family, and personal lives.

Being Questions

The key questions for being are more difficult than those for creating success. The first, Who am I?, has been asked by humans for as long as we have had words. The process of wrestling with this question is vexing and engaging, because it has no unalterable answer—it must be continually asked throughout our lifetimes.

Several spin-off questions follow, each revolving around a central theme of purpose. These spin-offs include: What gives meaning to my existence? What are my most deeply held values? What makes me unique? Why am I here? These questions also help us to know who we are. The clearer we can respond to them, the more we will be able to find balance between creating success and finding meaning.

Being Attitudes and Beliefs

The first attitude or belief necessary for being is *integrity*, which centers around truth and honesty. The closer the outer expression and inner feeling are to being the same, the more we can say that that person or organization has integrity. To put it differently, integrity is "finding the way of life and of being that will be true to its own nature."[4] Unfortunately, when most politicians say anything to get elected and corporate leaders are paid outlandish sums independent of the performance of their organizations, we might conclude that integrity, though talked about frequently, is not as common as we'd like it to be.

The second attitude or belief of being is *appreciation*—loving ourselves and others in the here and now, regardless of our accomplishments, acknowledging our uniqueness, separateness, and eventual mortality. Many of us would like to remain young forever; in our denial, we sometimes fail to appreciate the glory and wonder of simply being alive.

The third attitude or belief related to being has to do with being in the moment, being present for whatever it is we are experiencing at the time. Because we so often reminisce about the past, live vicariously through heroes or heroines, or dream about a utopian future, we risk missing the beauty of the eternal now. We rarely take the time for solitude and quiet; it is typically in times of crisis or trauma that we face ourselves in the moment.

Being Knowledge, Skills, and Abilities

The knowledge, skills, and abilities of being are subtle, resting largely on our capacity for quiet and to hear truths and wisdom that resonate within us, even though it is difficult for some or may make some anxious. But because I believe that virtually all we need to know resides inside of us, these skills are vital for our growth and well-being in the years ahead.

34   The first specific skill is knowing how to identify and clarify our most deeply held values and to understand the differences between our needs and wants. By "needs and wants," I am referring not simply to such issues as money, power, prestige, status, or even the more profound issues of challenge or contribution. Rather, I am referring to what is found after much inner searching, often in response to questions like, What are you willing to die for?, and As your final words, you have enough energy left to communicate one or two profound messages—what would they be? The answers to these questions are often difficult to know and to speak about, but as the French writer Marie Cardinal put it, "Until you learn to name your ghosts and baptize your hopes, you have not been born; you are still the creation of others."[5]

Parallel to this skill is our capability of accepting and owning our fears, defenses, and anything else about ourselves we consider bad, shameful, or needing to be kept from our awareness. These *shadow* parts of ourselves, to use Jungian terms, are not only integral to who we are but offer richness and wisdom by which we can move toward a greater sense of balance. Lest we think this is a skill for individuals only, organizations also have shadow sides—and one of the surest ways to get into trouble in your workplace is to name any of these out loud or point them out to those in power. It is my belief that our individual and societal reluctance to know and wrestle with these parts of ourselves is a profound reason why we find it virtually impossible to find any real sense of wholeness and peace in our lives, families, communities, and workplaces.

Methods and Techniques for Being

For Individuals

- Make time for quiet every day, whether it be formal meditation, prayer, or sitting at your desk gazing out the window.
- Keep a journal or diary where you can record your deepest thoughts and feelings.
- Spend time with friends, counselors, therapists, or others with whom you can be supported, encouraged, and even guided into the deeper parts of yourself.

For Couples and Families

- Follow all of the suggestions for individuals, shared with one another.
- Spend time together during which you do nothing and are completely quiet.
- Go on occasional retreats together, especially those that practice silence.
- Take vacations together that focus on trust-building experiences, such as those that require physical or mental challenges and joint effort and energy.

For Groups and Organizations

- Provide quiet rooms for thinking and achieving calm, open and accessible to everyone.
- Offer and support sabbaticals and similar leave arrangements.
- Promote weekly, monthly, and quarterly closure activities that encourage members to acknowledge and appreciate themselves and one another.
- Build quiet and appreciation time into all training and development processes.

Connecting

Connecting has to do with the interactions we have with others and the world around us. Connecting is centered on the quality of our interactions and recognizes that we need both deep and abiding relationships and a place where we have a sense of belonging in order to move toward a sense of balance. Connecting also reminds us that all things are interconnected and that we are mutually dependent on one another. Much of the "connecting" is superficial and insufficient to create the relationships necessary for any real sense of balance in our work, families, and personal lives.

Though many acknowledge the importance of connecting, many of us have not made this a significant part of our lives: We may be "too busy"; we may hesitate to move toward closeness or intimacy with others; we may only think longingly about friendships and nature, about doing things to improve our communities, but fail to take the challenge of actually doing something, for any number of good reasons. This basic lack of connecting, of groundedness, is a powerful deterrent to our health and happiness; without it balancing is simply not possible.

Connecting Questions

The first connecting question is the most critical: How do I create and nurture the relationships necessary for my vision and purpose? If we focus only on the success side of the equation, we are again talking about networking, about situational and short-lived relationships, about organizations that continually restructure in search of lowest costs or cheapest labor. It is only when we tack on the "finding meaning" part that we begin to understand connecting, because then we begin to form real friendships, build solid communities, and recognize the importance of supporting the environment in sustainable ways.

Connecting Attitudes and Beliefs

The first attitude or belief of connecting is *cooperation*, giving proper regard to the life, rights, and well-being of others. Although as children we are taught to share, get along with others, and give without getting, as adults we often cooperate only to the degree that we get what we want. Yet participative management, self-managing work teams, shared governance, and other innovations reflect a growing recognition that cooperation has much more to offer than simply getting along with one another.

Compassion is the second attitude or belief of connecting. If we are to connect with other people, then we must care about other people. Think of the compassion felt for a small child who falls down a well, yet how difficult it can be to demonstrate the same level of caring for family members, co-workers, or the less fortunate in our communities. Compassion for those closest to us and for strangers can lead to connections that will enrich our lives.

Trust is the third attitude or belief of connecting—letting others be free to be who they are, supporting their vision and purpose, and accepting it whether we understand it or not. Without trust, we will never know how we stand with one another, and this is a sure way to remain imbalanced.

The last attitude or belief of connecting is the valuing of *differences*, whether this be honoring and caring for our elders, hiring disabled workers into our organizations, or living and working in truly racially or culturally mixed communities.

As we move closer toward multicultural diversity, those who cannot see the value of these differences will find themselves increasingly on the outside looking in. The synergy that is possible when we bring our differences to bear on common problems is vital and necessary if we are to effectively wrestle with the challenges we are facing in the modern world.

Connecting Knowledge, Skills, and Abilities

The most important skill for connecting is knowing how to communicate effectively, whether in writing or orally, using any number of appropriate methods to send and receive messages and information. Effective communication begins and ends with the ability to listen. We all need to know and practice the basics of active listening—summarizing, reframing, and sending messages back to the receiver in positive terms. Knowing how to assert ourselves properly, learning other languages (not necessarily spoken ones), and being able to listen without having to respond are also essential for connecting.

Another important part of connecting comes under the heading of group process skills. As we work and live in closer proximity to more and more people, often with great urgency and not always with a lot of time to get to know one another, conflict resolution, negotiation, consensus, and team-building skills become increasingly important. These require assertiveness and sensitivity, and force us to look at our assumptions and prejudices about others and new situations. If we are to connect and reach some sense of common ground, our ability to work together will grow in value and importance.

The third skill refers to a capacity to connect ideas, data, symbols, and core properties from one realm to another. It includes the ability

38 to perceive and understand larger patterns even when key pieces of information are missing. This ability to conceptualize will become a fundamental skill in the years ahead.

Methods and Techniques for Connecting

For Individuals

- Learn and practice how to listen.
- Learn another language, whether spoken, written, artistic, musical, technological, or anything else that teaches you how to think in other ways and how to translate fluidly from one point of view to another.
- Spend time in other communities and cultures, not just as a casual observer, but as if you were actually living there.
- Volunteer your time, energy, and expertise in supporting causes, ideas, or programs that you believe are important and are in alignment with your purpose and vision.
- Make time regularly to ponder your purpose in life and keep a record of these ruminations.
- Learn something new every day.

For Couples and Families

- Follow all of the suggestions for individuals, shared with one another.
- Learn and practice positive negotiating strategies, including conflict resolution and consensus-building techniques that lead toward win-win outcomes.
- Make time for physical contact, including hand holding, hugs, and other spontaneous expressions of touching and holding.
- Encourage and demonstrate your affection and appreciation for one another. Smile often at one another and communicate the following: "I like you," "I am proud of you," "I care about you."

- Recognize and reward community involvement by making volunteers high-profile members and by making this involvement an actual part of their job description and performance standards.
- Create systems and procedures that allow everyone open access to all but the most highly sensitive information.
- Make valuing diversity a core norm for everything the group or organization does and create ways for members to interact with one another on a regular and frequent basis.
- Develop programs to eliminate barriers for women, people of color, the physically challenged, and others who have historically been locked out. These programs should offer real opportunities to demonstrate capabilities and potential.
- Invest in family and community care initiatives that are not limited just to child or elder care, such as business/school partnerships, urban renewal projects, and environmental initiatives.

Acting

Acting is similar to navigating, but it involves doing on a deeper level. This has to do with how we fulfill our purpose, how we make contributions, and is often spoken of in terms of the legacy we want to leave when we die. Acting also reinforces navigating in order to emphasize that movement is the essence of generative balancing. Acting also reminds us that balancing takes continuous work and attention.

Acting also forms the ethical basis for generative balancing by making responsibility an explicit imperative in all our actions and behaviors. Because acting focuses on fulfilling our purpose, it emphasizes well-being for ourselves as the actors, as well as for those with whom we act. Behaving in this way requires a great deal of attention, and many people find that the urgencies of their day often overpower their capacity to move forward in this way. This alignment of both purpose and daily activity is one of our most urgent and difficult challenges.

Acting Questions

The key question for acting may already be obvious: How do I achieve my vision and purpose? Just as navigating was about vision, acting is about the joining of vision with purpose. Its key question forces individuals, families, and workplaces to see beyond their goals and to not let the behaviors, efforts, policies, and systems of the day overshadow the purposes to which they are committed. That our actions can focus on both goals and purpose will not be anything new to most readers, but for most of us and for most of our lives, the purpose side of the equation generally takes a backseat to the journey to success.

The second question—How do I achieve success and at the same time experience a sense of meaning and fulfillment?—implies that in whatever ways we define success, we can also experience meaning and fulfillment. This ability has less to do with the ultimate purpose or direction of our endeavors than with how we are able to realize that all our experiences are meaningful. All experience, therefore, is inherently purposeful.

Acting Attitudes and Beliefs

The first attitude or belief of acting is *responsibility*, or an accountability to own up to the efforts, results, and consequences of our actions. Without responsibility, many actions will be reactive ones, knowing that we may be long gone before the aftermath of our actions become known. Assuming responsibility for our actions ensures that others will not have to be left holding the bag, using precious energy and resources to clean up after us.

The next attitude or belief of acting is *courage*. Courage is the sustained commitment and effort to confront our fears, not knowing what the outcome will be; it is "not the absence of fear; it is the making of action in spite of fear, the moving out against resistance engendered by fear into the unknown and into the future."[6] Not only is courage necessary for acting responsibly, it is also one of the keys for balancing.

The next attitude or belief important for acting is *patience*, the calm feeling of waiting while not losing sight of the path and steps ahead. We are often in such a hurry to get somewhere, to make our mark, that we sometimes fail to appreciate the importance of moving forward more deliberately and with appropriate attention. We need to have the patience to understand that acting toward one's deeper purpose often takes a very long time.

The last attitude or belief of acting is *perseverance*, or the willingness to do what it takes for as long as is necessary in order to achieve our vision and purpose. Most people who have accomplished real greatness, those heroines and heroes who most inspire us, often say that perseverance was integral to their achievements.

Acting Knowledge, Skills, and Abilities

The knowledge, skills, and abilities of acting are in many ways similar to those of navigating. The first of these is the ability to *follow through* what has been started. This does not mean that we should rigidly adhere to any particular course of action or blind ourselves to the need for changing course. Rather, it is an inner sense of self-discipline and staying power and the drive to complete the tasks at hand or solve a problem that has been vexing us.

The second set of skills important for acting are *focus* and *concentration*. These skills help us to do one thing at a time and allow our attention to be in the moment with that particular experience, even when so many choices and decisions confront us each day that we are tempted to do everything at once. These acting skills are essential if we are to achieve a lasting sense of well-being.

The third skill area for acting builds on those in being—it is our ability to work through fears, defenses, and other internal barriers. In being, the skill was owning and accepting them; in acting, it is knowing how to work on them until they are integrated into who we are and serve us in pursuit of our purpose. This turns a weakness into a strength; it makes our weakness part of our ongoing human development plan.

Methods and Techniques for Acting

For Individuals

- Write a letter or make a telephone call to someone in power about something important to you. Do this regularly and frequently.

- Focus on whatever it is you are doing right now, stay conscious of your thoughts and feelings, and let go of thoughts of the outcome.
- Involve yourself in a cause that you strongly believe in, especially one having to do with making the world a better place for our children.

For Couples and Families

- Follow all of the suggestions for individuals, shared with one another.
- Begin building a family tree that includes such information as history and dates, myths and secrets. Let this be a complete picture of your family, and be sure to involve as many members as possible in this ongoing project.
- Find hobbies and activities that are of interest to all family members and participate in them regularly to ensure their priority in family life.
- Consider the possibility of seeing and working with a therapist if difficulties arise in articulating or moving toward your shared purpose.

For Groups and Organizations

- Regularly examine policies, systems, and procedures to see how and if they support the stated vision and purpose. Create mechanisms for changing them if and when necessary.
- Create reward systems that recognize efforts and consequences, as well as results of performance. This may lead to a complete rethinking of your reward and compensation process.
- In addition to the usual quarterly and annual plans, develop ten-, twenty-, thirty-year plans, and even plans for the end of the next century.
- Hire and support an organizational adviser/mentor, whose charter is to help the organization and its members see themselves as they really are, not as they wish themselves to be. Be willing to support this person's recommendations if, on reflection, they make sense, even if contrary to much of how you've done business in the past.

In Summary

Finding meaning is the ultimate challenge for many individuals, families, and workplaces. As we have put more emphasis on creating success throughout our history, we have found ourselves imbalanced when it comes to finding meaning. Since our primary societal rewards—money and power—accrue to the successful, most of our time is devoted to success. Furthermore, finding meaning for most of us is a long-term proposition, and we have a history in our society of giving in to the short-term payoffs in lieu of the sacrifices often required to find real meaning.

Perhaps even more to the point is that finding meaning requires a commitment of a different order than that required for creating success. Finding meaning is about our inner experiences, how we feel about ourselves, and often requires us to look at painful areas of that inner world. The real dilemma is that all this work may or may not have any payoff in the outer world. Since most of us are not taught how to do this work, we often find ourselves fully grown and successful, and yet questioning important areas of our lives. Many of my clients, when they begin working on this deeply personal level, often speak of how much like little children they feel on the inside.

But as individuals and families begin to work more in the realm of finding meaning, they often are willing to make big changes to make meaning more central in their lives and work. From changing careers because they can no longer tolerate the emptiness or mindlessness of their jobs to simply bringing a different attitude to the very same work, as people tap into their need for meaning, they are forever changed. While finding meaning is rarely a result of those blinding flashes of insight, the search for it is compelling even for those who have always been driven by their need and desire for creating success.

In contrast to the individuals, couples, and families who are wrestling with finding meaning in their work and lives, organizations and their leaders are reluctant participants, at best. Many of the words and concepts in this chapter are integral parts of many organizational mission statements, but inspiring as these statements can be, as the

44 vagaries of a capricious marketplace wear on, most organizations back off on these so-called softer commitments. Employees in these organizations quickly sense the gap between the words and deeds; once this realism becomes part of the culture, it becomes a monumental task to bring balance into those workplaces.

Generative balancing posits that we need both sides of the equation, creating success and finding meaning, if we are to achieve any lasting individual well-being and workplace effectiveness. One of our great challenges will be to bring both of these together.

5

Renewal

The third competency of generative balancing is our will and capacity for renewal. Renewal is being able to see each day as new—to act as if this day is the only one there is. As figure 1 earlier showed, renewal is the fulcrum upon which the other two parts of the model rest, providing the energy necessary for those competencies—creating success and finding meaning—to emerge. As such, renewal is at the heart of the model; though invisible in everyday life, it is at the same time the spirit of who we are.

Renewal, as the unifying force of the model, is not divisible into components as are the other two. It does, however, have three defining characteristics. The first has to do with transition, or our capacity to adapt fluidly to changing circumstances. Transitions, while often being outwardly observable, do not usually imply deeper changes in who we are. A job change, a move to a new location, or the introduction of a new product to the marketplace are examples of such transitions. Some transitions are planned for; others just happen to us. Transitions often can be wrenching, especially to our routines, sometimes to our self-esteem, but they generally do not call into question our fundamental assumptions about who we are or why we are here.

Transformation, the second characteristic of renewal, is both the process and experience of deep change, in which who we are and how

46   we see, feel, and think about the world and our place in it becomes fundamentally different. Many aspects of our lives have characteristics of transition and transformation in the same experience, and there is rarely a clear distinction between the two. Transformations, whether by choice or by accident, are usually not easily assimilated or willingly integrated into our lives. A spinal cord injury leaving one paralyzed is transforming, just as are the couple who has just had their first child or the chief executive who is forced into retirement reluctantly. In each case, transformation usually requires significant psychological effort in letting go of and mourning the past, as well as beginning to embrace whatever the new may hold.

The third, most subtle characteristic of renewal is transcendence, an embracing of all our moments fully with complete awareness. This often leads to a connection with the divine and forms the core for nearly all religious and mystical traditions. Few experience this state other than for brief or fleeting moments, and for most, transcendence is more a by-product of practicing renewal rather than a specific goal in itself. When we do experience moments of transcendence, we experience a sense of oneness, wholeness, grace, love, and emanation.

Figure 4 details the specific questions, attitudes and beliefs, and knowledge, skills, and abilities of renewal.

Renewal Questions

The preeminent question of renewal is, How do I build the well-being of future generations into my own vision and purpose? This question alone could transform how we live and work. It forces us to make a link between the past and future through our actions and behaviors in the present. As you will see in the following interview chapters, it is a deep and abiding concern in many people's lives.

Another, no less important, renewal question, and a necessary complement to the first, is How do I access and use my creative, intuitive, and spiritual potential? These parts of ourselves are often suppressed, yet creativity and intuition have recently become acceptable in business. Spirituality, on the other hand, is still fairly taboo in

Attributes	
Questions	How do I build the well-being of future generations into my own vision and purpose? How do I access and use my creative, intuitive, and spiritual potential?
Attributes and Beliefs	Embrace the process of change Wonder Sense of perspective Love
Knowledge, Skills, and Abilities	Understanding of transition process Heartiness skills Ability to access and use creative, intuitive, and spiritual processes

Figure 4   Renewal

most circles of power, although spiritual needs and concerns often come pouring out in my talks in private with business leaders. By asking ourselves this question, perhaps we can bring it out in the open so that we can all work on it together.

Renewal Attitudes and Beliefs

Renewal's attitudes or beliefs are not only among the most difficult to internalize but are also often the most difficult to speak about. The first of these is embracing the process of change. This includes respecting and appreciating the rhythms of nature and life, including those in our everyday lives and work. Instead of ignoring, denying, or running from change, the renewing individual, family, or workplace willingly and consciously meets change openly and works to respond appropriately.

The next attitude or belief important for renewal is a sense of wonder and awe, the innocence, curiosity, and playfulness needed to create the foundation for hopefulness. To be able to experience each sunset as remarkable, to sit at the seashore mesmerized by the waves' endless rhythms, to cry uncontrollably at the birth of a child or the death of a loved one—all are essential to our health, well-being, and sense of renewal.

The third attitude or belief for renewal has to do with humility and having a sense of perspective of one's place in the universe and the grand scheme of things, recognizing how small and insignificant we really are. It also implies a willingness to accept the unknown and unknowable, coming to grips with our mortality and the mysteries of life. It is my belief that developing this attitude across our culture would go a long way toward helping us become a wiser, more compassionate nation.

The fourth on this list is the point of energy from which we all emanate, the profound and fundamental notion called love, the force permeating every word, concept, idea, and notion that we have. With love, we have unlimited possibilities. As we find ways to make love more explicit in our work, families, and personal lives, we will grow immeasurably and come closer to the embrace of renewal.

Renewal Knowledge, Skills, and Abilities

The first of renewal's knowledge, skills, and abilities is a cluster involving knowledge and understanding of the various ways we grow, change, let go, and move on. The more we understand about the stages of grieving, for example, or understand the commonalities of all human change, the more we will be able to guide our transitions and transformations, both in terms of timing them well and getting the most from those experiences. Our recognition that the endings and beginnings in our lives are interspersed with times of upheaval and oscillation between the old and the new helps us to not feel bad or strange when we go through these all-too-human experiences. As we begin to understand and internalize these ideas, our transitions and transformations will be more likely to serve us well.

The second area has to do with heartiness skills. When we have the strength, flexibility, stamina, sensitivity, and energy to move through our days fluidly and with energy, we are more likely able to keep our vision and purpose alive. Vigorous exercise, regular stress management, play, proper nutrition, and expression of sexuality are means by which we sensitize ourselves and bring ourselves closer to renewal; we are more able to make contact with the divine and feel its presence. Heartiness is associated with a fundamental respect for our physical bodies and attention to our physical essence. Our bodies thus become another conduit for making connection with the divine.

The third area is ability to use creative, intuitive, and spiritual potential for renewal. Our creative potential allows us to see the familiar in new ways or to imagine the new from nothing. This capacity is a defining human characteristic that can help us move toward balance. Courses in creativity are almost becoming routine in traditional MBA programs, and creative thinking is now woven into a number of innovative management training programs. As we learn how to think more creatively, we will become much more able to tackle the complex and entrenching problems of the world today.

Intuition is an ability to know without data, information, or conscious thinking. That virtually all decision makers use some degree of intuition is rarely acknowledged in our show-me-the-evidence-before-I-decide culture. One of the best ways to train ourselves to use our intuition is to place ourselves in unfamiliar situations—jobs, new relationships, new cultures—that call on us to make quick and good decisions. Intuition can be cultivated during times of quiet, then listening for messages that rise from deep within.

Spirituality makes people nervous when talked about openly—partly because of the connection with religion and partly because of the ambiguity of its meaning. Yet well over half the hundreds of individual clients I have seen in past years have spoken of spirituality as a deep and guiding force in their lives and about their need to bring spirituality into their work and personal lives. Those who report the most positive outcomes are those who find ways to integrate their spirituality into their work and lives.

For most of us, doing this is not really all that difficult if we can only develop the discipline. Most important is that spirituality be practiced and that it become a part of the fabric of how we live and work each day.

50   Methods and Techniques for Renewal

For Individuals

- Laugh whenever you feel the urge.
- Make time for play. Recognize that if it is hard, then it's not really play.
- Develop and practice a regular spiritual regimen.
- Exercise regularly, but not obsessively.
- Read inspiring stories about others who have persevered through major difficulties and who have mastered change.
- Learn and practice alternative ways for expressing yourself. For example, compose poetry, write and sing songs, dance in the rain, play a musical instrument, or finger paint.

For Couples and Families

- Follow all of the suggestions for individuals, shared with one another.
- Spend time together in silence.
- Create and enact rituals for letting go and moving on that include those that allow for mourning and grieving, and those that celebrate turning points and transitions.

For Groups and Organizations

- Create ways for members to learn about and study the future, including trend watching, forecasting, and designing alternative futures for the enterprise.
- Offer help, assistance, or training to the survivors of restructuring and other big changes. This should, at the least, include stress management training, time and support for venting feelings, and a recognition that during transition, very few are immediately ready to return to business as usual.
- Create and implement wellness programs that focus on such issues as stress management, nutrition, drug education, exercise, and preventive health practices.

- Build development and reward systems that value and promote creative, intuitive, and spiritual leadership styles and processes. This should begin with the top leadership of the group or organization.

In Summary

Renewal takes place within and affects everything about what we do and who we are. Though the process is not directly visible, when we are renewing ourselves, we have the capacity for bringing subtle and defining characteristics into creating success and finding meaning. Renewal is the integrating force of generative balancing and gives us the power to move fluidly and appropriately from one end of the spectrum to the other between creating success and finding meaning. When we can move easily between these two and know when to do so, our acts and behaviors, ideas, thoughts, and feelings radiate a sense of wholeness and completeness.

For our personal and family lives, renewal means that work, important though it may be, should not consume us, and even when it does, we must remember that it is still only one aspect of our lives, rarely a life-or-death situation. It means that we value and learn from all relationships, even those that may be tedious and difficult. We are able to see others as filled with their own unique potential and always having something to offer us. It means that we have a deep and abiding respect for all life, including our enemies. We remember to take time out from our toils to appreciate our lives, whatever our circumstances may be.

For organizations and workplaces, renewal means that profits, sales, market share, and other success measures are tempered by paying attention to the quality of relationships, building integrity throughout the business, and working toward adding value to all aspects of society. It means that buzzwords like *excellence*, *quality*, and *best* are used only when the daily experiences of employees reflect those characteristics. And it means that organizations must make serious, visible, and long-term commitments to the well-being of future generations, not

52 as an afterthought but as an integral part of why and how they do business.

Most of all, renewal brings awareness of living in the here and now. It is from this place, whether at work or play, that we are simultaneously grounded and connected with the divine. These times might be rare in our busy lives, or even irrelevant, but it is during these renewing moments that we are most alive and most able to be all of who we are. This means that we have greater access to truth and wisdom, and today we need all that we can muster. As we build renewal into our lives and work, we move toward greater balance.

Time Out for Balancing

This is the first of two time-outs in this book, each intended to take you away from reading for a moment and into the process of balancing. This first time-out can be done quickly or slowly, all at once or in segments, as time allows.

Some may find it easier to have another person read the time-out to them, making it easier to engage the process. Or you may want to record the instructions, then play them back, following them at a pace that works for you. However you go through this exercise, it is important to find a time and place where you will not be interrupted and where you are able to put all other thoughts and concerns aside for the time being. Put yourself into as relaxed a state as possible. A place to record your experiences may prove useful. With that in mind, let's begin.

Imagine that you are about to begin a journey that will bring you to a place of peace, calm, and most of all, a sense of fulfillment. This does not necessarily mean that you will get or achieve everything you seek, but rather it will be a place where you feel complete and whole. Take a few moments (or longer, if you like) to experience whatever images, sensations, thoughts, and feelings are coming to you as you begin your journey....

Before proceeding, take some additional time to consider the following questions:

- What are you experiencing right now?
- What questions, issues, and concerns confront you as you begin your journey?
- Who goes with you and who stays behind?
- What skills will help you and what will you need to learn along the way?
- What will be a good pace of travel for you and how will you know that?

You begin your journey full of energy and enthusiasm, eager to experience what lies ahead. You find the early going easy and smooth and yet somehow not quite up to your expectations.... You are moving ahead at a steady pace, but somewhere inside, you are aware that something isn't quite right.... Again, take as much time as you need to experience how the journey is for you right now....

Before proceeding, take some time to ponder the following questions:

- How are you feeling right now?
- What have been the high points of your journey so far?
- What are some of the obstacles, barriers, and difficulties you have encountered? What have you done about them? What have you learned?
- Something about your journey isn't quite right for you at this point.... What is it?

Back to the journey, and you are further along still...now moving confidently, powerfully, with a strong sense of clarity and purpose...when all of a sudden, a major tragedy befalls you and stops you in your tracks. Use your imagination to experience what that might be and allow yourself to feel deeply the impact it has on you. (If you are having difficulty thinking of a tragic event in your journey, you may want to consider one of the following possibilities: divorce or breakup of a significant relationship, a life-threatening illness for you or your loved ones, death of anyone close to you, betrayal of someone you trusted, or financial setbacks.) Give yourself plenty of time to be with the experience and your feelings, and do not move on until you have thoroughly engaged this part of the journey....

Before proceeding, take some time to ponder the following questions:

- How are you feeling right now?
- How has this event slowed or modified your journey?
- In what ways has it changed your perspective?
- What lessons do you derive for the remainder of the journey?
- How will you regain the energy, enthusiasm, and momentum to continue?

You can sense now that you are coming near to the end of the journey.... You feel solid and your pace is naturally beginning to slow down.... You find that others are coming to you for advice, ideas, and inspiration.... You also know, deep inside, that the journey is not yet over, that there are still experiences, lessons, beauties, and joys that await you.... Allow yourself as much time as you want to feel this expansive, generative place....

Before proceeding, take some time to ponder and reflect on the following questions:

- How are you feeling right now and how are those feelings similar or dissimilar to those in other parts of the journey?
- As you look back, what recollections and memories do you have?
- What words do you have for those who are seeking your advice?
- How will you help them understand the nature of the journey?
- What regrets do you have, and which of those have been or are still difficult to let go of?

Your journey is now very near the end.... You can feel it in your heart, mind, and body.... You are saddened and nostalgic for losses, but you are also lighter, more playful, and wiser than you have ever been.... You have let go of your need to achieve and you can just be.... Just as the lights go dark, you feel the most sublime sense of aliveness....

56

- What are you experiencing right now?
- What words, images, or symbols most accurately capture that experience?
- What messages do you hear, see, or feel?

After pondering these last questions, stay quiet for a while longer and experience whatever it is that may be going on for you.... In doing so, spend some time contemplating the following questions:

- What ideas can you bring back with you on how to live your life in the present moment?
- How will you make those a part of your work, family, and personal life?

Now that you have finished this time-out, you may want to revisit all or parts of it on a regular basis, and add to or modify it as you do so. It might also be fun to share your experience with others, or, perhaps, do the exercise in a family, group, or work setting. With others, you are likely to have an intense and powerful process, one that will potentially be moving for all who choose to participate.

Before going on to part 2, set this book down for a while. Let the ideas and concepts from part 1 and the experience of this time-out sink in and become a part of you. And as you move forward in this book and your life, do what you can to stay aware of the learnings and experiences you have gathered so far.

Balancing in Daily Life

So we are coming to a conception of happiness that differs fundamentally from the storybook version. The storybook conception tells of desires fulfilled; the truer version involves striving toward meaningful goals—goals that relate the individual to a larger context of purposes. Storybook happiness involves bland idleness; the truer conception involves seeking and purposeful effort. Storybook happiness involves every form of pleasant thumb twiddling; true happiness involves the full use of one's powers and talents. Both conceptions of happiness involve love, but the storybook version puts great emphasis on being loved, the truer version on the capacity to give love.

—John W. Gardner

Self-Renewal: The Individual and the Innovative Society

6

Individuals Balancing

The people you will meet in this chapter are single or separated from their partner or, if in an ongoing relationship, the nature of the interview was that they spoke from an individual point of view. Their ages ranged from early thirties into the seventies. Regardless of age, gender, or ethnic background, there were a number of striking similarities in their stories.

Some of these themes will be obvious and others may be less so. I hope that as you read these interviews, as well as those in following chapters, you can imagine yourself listening to them just as I did, nodding your head in agreement with a number of the people here. As you read, pay attention to any thoughts, feelings, impressions, and images that come to you. You may want to keep a journal of your reactions and perhaps make notes of how you and the interviewee see balancing in similar or different ways.

Lydia DeMille

Single parent, two teenage daughters, works full-time, in the midst of making a career change

Lydia's story is similar to those of many other single parents working to ensure the best possible life for themselves and their children. She faces some new challenges as she works through a career change, but her parenting responsibilities have lightened somewhat now that her children have reached adolescence and attained a certain level of independence. She recounts her efforts at balancing as follows:

"Most of balancing for me has to do with organizing my time, getting my priorities straight, and figuring out what I can and cannot do. As the parent of two teenage daughters, both of whom are quite independent and supportive of my current endeavors, I finally feel that now I have some time for myself. It's my time now! Even though all three of us are busy with jobs and school, I try to focus on the moment by taking one step at a time.

"Even though there are days when things go wrong no matter what I do, right now things pretty much feel in balance. I have more energy than I used to and am less tired. I feel really good, sort of like being on a natural high. When things are going well for me like this, it's like a light dawns for me!

"I've learned that when things get out of balance for me, the thing I can do is assert myself, saying, 'This is what I want,' then try to follow through by following my own advice. If this gets hard or confusing, I try just to hang in there until things get clear.

"I take things as they come and when things get tough, like recently when all of our cars broke down at the same time, I try to keep a good attitude. Instead of getting angry or upset, I look to see the funny side of things.... When this doesn't work, I remind myself and the kids that we'll get through this!

"I used to believe in the 'perfect family,' but my friends and I have had to give up this idea. We need to redefine just what a family is, and when we get together our conversations often go to the question of, By the time we were forty, didn't we think life would be easier? Our lives are anything but easy and nothing like we envisioned them to be!

"I want others to know that a positive attitude is so important...and this means being flexible and taking things as they come. We also need to accept the fact that we can't really control the future. Often when things get particularly out of hand, I like to say and to hear, 'I am proud of you.' With that one statement, ten days of aggravation can be wiped out instantly."

Lydia embodies generative balancing in several ways. Her positive attitude, which came through both in her words and her tone of voice, symbolizes one of the key features of generative balancing—valuing positive and life-affirming attitudes and beliefs. She also has the ability to be in the moment, to be present with whatever she is doing at the time. She conveyed one of renewal's attributes with her sense of perspective and her capacity to see things as they are. Perhaps most importantly, she laughed a lot throughout our interview, and in so doing conveyed a sense that at least for now she is approaching balance with pleasure and gusto.

Bob Noone

Lives alone, works a traditional job, and has recently started a business buying and selling classical records

Bob doesn't face the same kind of daily stresses as Lydia and other single parents, but he confronts other issues no less pressing. Among these are deriving a sense of meaning when there is not the intimacy offered by partners or children. Listen to what Bob has to say:

"For me, balancing has to do with healing and is the biggest act of freedom I can give myself. I frequently check in with myself by asking, 'What do I feel like doing now?' Balancing is then a question of being fully present with whatever I'm doing or with whomever I'm with. It also has to do with making time available, letting go of parental messages, and managing my life so that I get what I want. A large part of what I want is time just to be…time to sit by a stream listening to water run over the rocks…time to listen to my music.

"When I'm in balance, I'm in touch with my feelings and very aware of what is happening around me. I also feel very vulnerable, which I see as a positive part of my life, and open to taking it all in. Balance is a sense of peacefulness and is a nonverbal and intuitive experience that is much like the sensuality of my music.

"I've been doing a lot of work on myself for many years and for the longest time I couldn't cry or get angry. Recently, though, I've been able to experience a much fuller range of feelings.... Though much of this has been painful, my ability to experience joy and intimacy has expanded greatly.... It is a gift!

"There is another piece of balancing and that has to do with accessing my power. When I need to make a decision, I've learned it is important to sit awhile and wait. The answers come, if I make time for quiet, and these are usually in sync with my values. By doing this, I also have space inside to check in and ask myself, What is important? This is, of course, an ongoing process, where I am constantly making choices. I find that my decisions are usually the appropriate ones.

"For balancing to be made easier, first of all our leaders must get their own houses in order. Those same leaders should look toward participatory governance, and peace and justice should be our core values. We must all get beyond our denial and look inside. Also, television distorts the real value of human beings and has in many ways devastated the family. Other than having some high-quality stereo equipment for listening to my music, I have little use for technology.

"Before we finish, I want to remind you of the power of the Serenity Prayer, which goes, 'God grant me the serenity to accept the things I cannot change, the courage to change the things I can, and the wisdom to know the difference.' Also, my growing realization of how little control I have over things has been both humbling and freeing. It allows me to laugh easily and lovingly at myself and has opened for me a pathway to my spiritual and higher power."

Bob has embraced finding meaning, and he continues to devote considerable time and energy to working through a number of obsessions. Though this is often painful for him, he recognizes that living this way is both energizing and a more healthy way for him to live. He also believes strongly that until our cultural norms begin to allow for more balance, we are all in for some difficult times ahead. Bob's enthusiasm during our interview reminded me that balancing is not about arrival at any one place, but it is a lifelong unfolding of who we are and living in the moment as much as possible.

Camille Harker

Single parent with older children, going through a major career transition

Camille, like Lydia, is confronted with parenting, working, and completing a degree program that will lead her to a new career. She recognizes that balancing is difficult and that while she has many of the bases well covered, there are areas of her life that are not in balance. Here is her story:

"Balancing is about trying to give something valuable to each area of my life. I find this hard to do, though, partly because of the residual guilt I feel for not being there when my kids were younger, and also in wanting to do everything well. I often compare myself to others and see that I can't get it all done—things like journal writing, which I consider important.

"I see several areas where balancing is a real challenge for me. First is that I made a bad career move recently and my job is both stressful and made even more difficult by a boss who comes from the Dark Ages. I'm also going to school for a new career, and because of the time demands, I have less flexibility and am less able to get things done. I'd also like to have a significant other in my life, but so far that person has not appeared. I am way out of balance in this area! Money, as with many other single mothers, used to be a real problem, but it's not so much anymore now that my kids have gotten older.

"I have a number of ideas that would help people to achieve better balance. First, we need to accept that there are no norms anymore and that things like telecommuting and working at home are trends that need to be supported. Organizations need to find nontraditional ways to compensate their employees, such as through sabbaticals and time off to develop other areas of their lives. Organizations could also do what mine has done—instead of laying off employees, do an across the board, enforced reduction in paid work hours. Daycare is important and things like fitness centers, a library, lounge facilities, along with giving employees time to use these, would also be helpful. Lunchtime gatherings and workshops, not all of which have to be related to work, are something else to consider.

"We all need to try to find the time to bring more balance into our lives. Developing a sense of community, where people share responsibility, is important. Also, we need to look at our priorities so that we can establish what is important in our lives. Once this is done, the rest of the pieces will fall into place. I know this is not easy and that priorities tend to shift over time, but we can be flexible. Lastly, imagine that this is the last day of your life.... This will help put things in perspective and show us what is important during the time we have."

Camille embodies an important part of renewal with the closing statement in our interview. She is somewhat caught up with her need to do everything well, which, though important in creating success, makes it harder for her just to be. Her sense of balance revolves around doing, and this presents her with other challenges. Camille could perhaps begin to scale back on her task orientation, along with her perfectionistic tendencies, and then perhaps some of the heaviness I sensed from her in the interview would be lifted.

Dave Boudreau

Divorced and works full-time, much of it from an office in his home

Dave is at a time in his life when he is giving careful consideration to the notion of balance. Even before we talked, he had given thought to writing on the subject himself, and it was obvious from the moment we began our conversation that he would have a lot to say. Here are his words:

"Balanced is a place I'd like to be! Sometimes work is such a main feature of my life, I often wonder, Why is it that work captures so much of my concern and attention? I guess there is a fine line between compulsion and passion, the former using me up and not leaving much, and the latter energizing me for work and everything else.

"It is important that I use my talents well in work that is worthwhile and makes a contribution. I also know that my relationship with my family is something to work on, and something else less specific, and hard to put into words, is a spiritual need that has been steadily growing in me since midlife. About six years ago, I went through what you might call a major panic or anxiety attack. I was in the midst of a lot of change, including a divorce, and it was for me a 'dark night of the soul.'

"I began to realize that the real issue was that I had no spiritual anchors.... My growing spiritual need has changed from that earlier anxiety to where today I feel a sense of awe about the infinity and abstraction of the spiritual dimension. I remind myself continuously that I did not create myself, that I came out of something else. Nothing has prepared me to deal with these ideas and I cannot escape from them...nor would I even want to at this point in my life. I try not to let work and other parts of my life get in the way of this abstract reality.

"When I do feel in balance, it's more like a flow rather than a plan.... My days look a little brighter...leading to a sense of inner joy. There really is time for everything and nothing really matters all that much! When I'm in balance, I just know things will be okay, and I experience both relaxation and energy, an inner ease, that I feel throughout my body.

"My mind often gets in the way, though, especially in my need to be productive and to generate a certain amount of income.... I would love to be able to work while in balance! I am well programmed to achieve and to do, but I have had very little programming about being.... I know that those who have had impact on me, it is out of their beingness.

"Balancing could be made if organizations would first begin moving toward an attitude of human resource appreciation and development, changing the bottom line from profits and quarterly reports to making a worthwhile contribution. It would also involve creating a nurturing environment where intelligence and creativity are continuously supported. On the home front, we need to realize that love is the central force in our lives and that play is one expression of love. We also need to have humor and joy in our lives and not let other things get in the way.

"It's also important that we begin to know our shadow, which is our willingness to experience the things we usually deny or repress. By making friends with this part of ourselves, we can open up to deep self-knowledge. This sense of opening up is for me a direct communication with my soul!"

Dave had much to say, especially in the realm of finding meaning. Although he is committed to his spiritual development, it is clear that he struggles to maintain balance between his work priorities and these other parts of himself. Dave also is willing to engage the tough questions posed earlier, and from what I could tell in our interview, he finds them to be challenging and energizing. Dave also had an inner sense of patience about this journey that I did not hear from many of the other interviews.

Sandy Croft

Married, no children, sole proprietor of a new business

Sandy is in this chapter because she chose to speak from a distinctly individual point of view. She does not have the same kinds of stresses and pressures that parents have, and she brings an almost other worldy perspective to the subject of balancing. Here is what she has to say:

"Balancing is not easy—it is an art.

"I define it as lovingly giving myself things and staying harmonized. When I am balanced, my thinking is diffused and I am more intuitive. Everything moves easily. I am energized, heart-centered, patient, and happy. I am really loving, and have more strength, more energy, and am more physically able to keep my balance. When I am out in nature, where my mind can relax, I enter into altered states, and I see patterns of energy and more of what there is…. I give myself permission to do nothing and to spend time in unstructured ways. I have no television set and where I put my attention is very important. I am very involved when working, but I take regular ten-minute catnaps that are renewing for me.

"Our culture teaches us to separate things and not see the whole picture—there is much more to our lives than most of us are aware of! I see tremendous discordance, a spiritual poverty, and people need to be connected with God to not feel so crazy. Its also important to become aware of and acknowledge that we are really scared, and not to react or create stuff out of fear. Instead, once we come face-to-face with our fears, we will have the faith and trust necessary to ask, What is our purpose?

"It is important to stay with the process. We are these mystical creatures, and the journey itself is balance. When in pain, we can use our learning ability and natural systems of change to seek another way. Also, we should stay with the process of questioning, seek out wise people, and read the classics. It's all there if we ask...."

I was impressed with Sandy's depth and sincerity. It is clear that her spiritual potential is a guiding force in her life. She also is explicit about connecting, especially to nature, which is obviously an important aspect of her spirituality.

Lanz Lowell

Single, no children, recently left his position in a large corporation to start a consulting practice

Lanz's interview reveals many of the themes we have already heard, but he has another issue that enters into the balancing equation. And like some of the others, he has spent considerable time pondering just what balancing means in his life. He says:

"When I think about balancing, my first response is that the cultural scale doesn't fit for me. It is more of a flow, where I circle around and check in, and knowing when to shift depending on what is going on inside and out. So it is not just equilibrium, not just doing more of one thing or less of something else. I focus on how I'm going to divvy up my time, recognizing that in the larger scheme of my whole life, there may be times to do a lot of one thing and less of another.

"My challenges revolve around having a mechanism to evaluate my sense of balance. For example, when I'm focused on my internal life, I need to ask myself, How do I make money? and conversely, when I'm out there making money, I ask, How do I slow down and stop? These questions are my biggest challenges. I keep the whole thing in perspective by asking a third question, How do I stay conscious about the choices I am making? By nurturing this spiritual side of who I am, I have the space to be reflective and to have the necessary clarity to make the right choices.

"I am HIV positive and this fact has acted as a kick in the pants for me. Being forced to confront my own death, I am much more aware of

68 the beauty around me and because of the immediate threat, I see every day as precious. I ask, Why am I here? and I try to live in a perfect way, which I define as living fully, communicating clearly, and doing what I want to do. By facing death, I am able to live more fully.... My life is intense, meaningful, sometimes confrontational.... With perhaps not as much time, I am living my life differently.

"When I am balanced, I have a lot of energy and feel a sense of integration. There is a freedom of movement that encompasses both the active and the quiet. It is not a middle ground so much as it is being clear enough so that my energy flows easily from me and out to those activities I choose. I feel a sense of connectedness, especially when meditating.

"Balancing is the most crucial topic we face, although I prefer the word *learning* as a more operative word. I also believe in the power and value of community rituals so that our seeking is not so dependent on us as individuals."

This interview with Lanz was intense and alive, and I felt his ability to move easily from his creating success mode to finding meaning. That he is forced to confront his own death at a much earlier age than most has given his life a certain sharpness that was powerful and engaging. As generative balancing suggests, we can all bring this same type of energy into our lives if we would only bring our mortality closer to us. Lanz's interview was filled with deep and probing questions, all of which are integral to generative balancing. And finally, Lanz recognizes the importance of community, especially as it relates to providing support for life's difficult times.

Judy Russell

Single parent with teenage children and with a job that involves extensive international travel

Judy, not unlike many other single parents, struggles with the demands of her work and the time she wants to spend with her children. Her kids are older now, but she wonders about what impact her career focus has had on their upbringing. Her story goes as follows:

"Balancing? Impossible! I travel a lot and I have often felt guilty for not being there for my kids. I am also angry at the work system where staying late for meetings and putting in the long hours is expected. Balancing for me is being the best mother I can be and also have a career. Though I experienced a lot of guilt when my kids were young, they remember me differently, and when I was there with them, I really was there!

"Balancing is extremely difficult for me. Because I am traveling as much as seventy percent of the time and my work doesn't stop just because I am not in the office, I am always running to catch up. My sleep patterns are disrupted and I feel tired most of the time. I do, however, try to spend time in silence because when I am silent, I feel centered and relaxed and I have a sure sense of my own values and morals.

"Balancing is having enough time to do what I want to do, and this does not include work. I like to think about when I was growing up on a farm: creative, staring at the ceiling, spending time with family, and feeling that time was endless. The way I want to be living is in the moment and being accepted for who I am.

"Some of the changes that would make balancing easier begin with the educational system. They should encourage more journal writing and have consciousness-raising classes and make the educational process more holistic and integrated. We all need to be asking about the relationship between family and society, with particular emphasis on what we are learning about the various roles each of us play in the society. I would like to see workplace support for parents becoming more active in the community and not having to feel guilty or deceptive to do that.

"My organization patterns its work style after how the chief executive does his work, and I think we should let go of that model. Instead, I'd like to see a norm something like, 'Trust that I will do suitable work in the way I want to do it.' I would also like to see more time and space for creativity. For me, this means time for silence and to do nothing. Also, there comes a time when we need to accept the gap between expectations and reality; for me, accepting this has allowed me to realize

70 that I am just an ordinary person, and I can be more relaxed and accepting of myself."

Judy touched on a number of areas that are crucial for generative balancing. She noted in several places how important and grounding silence is for her. This both serves as respite from her busy life and provides a time for reflection. She also spoke of acceptance and of being "ordinary," which are important for connecting and discovering. Of most significance, she spoke openly of her anger toward a system and culture that makes balancing so illusive for her. In so doing, she is not disowning her own responsibility for her situation, but recognizes that her own personal acting can only take her so far toward balancing.

Troy Hendrikson

Married, young children, owns his own business

Troy spoke to me directly and concretely, and as an African American man, he made it clear that there are many impediments to his achieving any real sense of balance. Here is his interview:

"Balancing has to do with the basic trials and tribulations of living, encumbered by the competitiveness of being a minority. I can't ever let go and relax, and just to tread water, I have to be ten feet tall and bazooka-proof. As an African American professional man, I feel I'm required to be twice as persistent, patient, and cunning to have any credibility when not part of the 'good ole boys' network. There is a necessity of having a sixth sense about people, and I often feel the need to go even further up to a tenth sense because of the pressures I experience.

"I have a number of ideas that would make balancing easier. First, I think there should be a much stronger collaboration among African American professionals. Currently we don't do this to the degree or at the level of sophistication of other ethnic groups. We have the resources, but we don't use them. Also, there needs to be meaningful opportunities for young people, where jobs are consistent with educational levels obtained. There also is a need for better technical training and vocational schools. I want to point out, too, that blacks, because we traverse several different worlds, have unique skills and stress-coping abilities that are particularly well suited for mid- and upper-level management.

"My advice to others begins with mind over matter, which means that much of what we worry about never happens. Everyone should use their talents, those qualities inside that often are not tapped. Learning something new every day helps us to understand ourselves and the world. Attitude is important…the first thing I do in the morning is reach over to my dresser and put on my rose-colored glasses…where my perception of the world becomes enthusiasm and working to meet people on common ground. Finally, I recommend maintaining a degree of calmness, having a good and wholesome family life, and respecting the rights of others."

Troy has spent a good deal of his life creating success, and he has the battle scars to prove it. He recognizes the importance of responsibility, and learning is obviously important to him. As his interview demonstrated, having a positive and life-affirming attitude is what makes all the difference in creating success and finding meaning.

Jocelyn Day

Divorced, young child, works part-time in a senior-level management position for a company that is floundering after several years of rapid growth

Jocelyn struggles with the demands of parenting and her own ambitions. She has learned to give more to her daughter, and she has gone through a number of changes, not the least of which was a failed marriage that could not withstand the intensity of this delicate balancing act. Here is her interview:

"The first thing that comes to my mind when I think about balance is stress! Each of these aspects of work, family, and personal life are all fluid and demanding. I'm the parent of a two-year-old, and prior to parenthood, work was my number-one priority. In fact, I've had to cut back on my work, because my life was becoming a series of problems…most notably my divorce. Having a child was the triple-bypass surgery I needed to shift my priorities!

"I went into marriage and parenthood with a cavalier attitude. Now providing some stability and consistency for my daughter is my highest priority. For me to be able to say, 'My life is important!' has been a big shift and my symbols of success are changing as a result. I have had to deal with problems of self-esteem and I can no longer avoid myself. Since I am still in the process of making this shift, I really don't know yet what balancing feels like!"

Jocelyn is in transition from an overemphasis on creating success to something that is not yet clear to her. It is obvious, though, that she has grown much in response to her recent pain, indicating that finding meaning is becoming a bigger part of her life. She still struggles with her perfectionism and finds it difficult to let go and get more deeply into things. She is, however, on the verge of moving into some new and deeper areas of her life.

Vince Santios

Single, no children, owns and operates his own consulting practice

Vince told me when we were scheduling our interview that he believed that once he got out of his "nine to five rut," balancing would be easier. He soon found out it wouldn't be quite that simple. Here is Vince:

"Balancing is just...rough, tough...difficult to do. Now that I am on my own, there is no structure and I have to be with myself much more of the time. I fly planes, and balancing is a lot like flying, where I am constantly using my visual flying rules, trusting what I am seeing and feeling, and being in sync with my skills.

"In my real life, this doesn't happen much, but when it does, it's like finding a center of gravity, like getting the plane up and flying level and I'm there! But in order to climb, I then have to overcome all the forces again, add power, break free, and rebalance. Balancing is not a static concept, but something much more dynamic.

"Spirituality is also part of the picture and I wonder just how does this thread work its way into my life? It is the tether that keeps it all together...it's there for accessing, but I seldom go to that place. You've got to work at it...plodding through...there's always more to learn. Teaching is a good way to find balance; you learn about yourself, and in the give and take that happens in good teaching, a spark happens!

"People should put on a backpack and go for a long hike to teach themselves about physical balance. We need adversity, challenge, to sit with tension...not flee, run, or fight, but keep engaged...the best of times come out of this!"

Vince recognizes that finding balance is a process filled with tension. He acknowledges that it is difficult to stay with it at times, but it is our willingness to "engage" that makes the difference for him. He exemplifies how heartiness and spirituality is an important aspect of renewal and the entire balancing process.

As this chapter comes to a close, I hope you will reflect on the words and stories shared by each of the interviewees. Some, as you saw, struggle with balance in their lives, probably like many of you. As I listened to each of them respond to my questions, I was struck again at the humanity of these people doing their best, trying to make wise decisions, often under great stress. That they are so honest about their lives and struggles, that they are willing to engage head-on their doubts and concerns about modern life, makes me hopeful that a greater degree of balance in work and life is truly possible.

Major Issues and Challenges for Individuals

1. Letting go of control is an important ingredient in balancing but very difficult to do.
2. There is not enough time to do everything and still have time left over for self or just for fun or doing nothing.
3. There is a lot of guilt for not paying enough attention or giving enough time to children, especially during their early years.
4. There is a sense of isolation and loneliness that comes from living alone and not having the time and energy to build intimate relationships.

74

5. There is a lack of support for single parents, including adequate and affordable childcare and flexible work schedules.
6. There is not enough time and energy for spiritual needs.
7. There is a tendency for people to be hard on themselves and overly critical for being less than perfect.
8. Learning is important, but this is often not as high a priority as many would like it to be.
9. Societal expectations and standards often complicate the need and desire to find greater balance in work and lives.

Strategies for Working Through the Issues and Challenges

1. Form or join support groups of others who share similar concerns and questions.
2. Take time for yourself, even if this means losing some sleep or working a few minutes less now and then.
3. Learn how to ask for help when feeling overwhelmed or out of control.
4. Become an advocate for childcare initiatives at local, state, and national levels. Talk to bosses, write to legislators.
5. Turn off the television set and use that time in other productive or meaningful ways.
6. Learn how to say no. Practice this regularly, even if it is occasionally a risky thing to do.
7. Begin a regular spiritual practice.
8. Find simple ways to bring levity and lightness into your life and work.
9. Become involved with community-building projects that resonate with your vision and purpose.

7

Couples and Families Balancing

The people you will meet in this chapter are members of couples or families. As you will see, any one of them could just as easily have fit into the previous chapter. They have been included here specifically because the couple/family relationship is central to them, and much of the interview spoke of that relationship. Many of their balancing issues and challenges are similar to those expressed by the earlier interviewees, but they are made complicated by the dynamics inherent in any intimate, ongoing relationship.

Families have undergone profound transformation in recent years, and however we look at or think about these changes, one thing I conclude is that there are few guiding principles today. Millions of people are trying to adapt to all that is changing in their lives, and are looking for ways to lead satisfying, productive, and happy family lives. That families are less permanent, that so many new and different arrangements are emerging and being tried, that the roles between men and women, whether in parenting or simply living as a couple, are transforming, and that so many lament the loss of past simple times, in no way diminishes the yearning for balance that so many couples and families are seeking.

Chris Panulti

Married, six children, both she and her husband work in full-time, demanding careers

Chris and her husband have a blended family, in which they both have children from previous marriages. She wrestles with having time and energy left for herself and her husband after the job and kids have been taken care of. Here is what she has to say:

"My husband and I have six children, three families: his, mine, and ours. We are a normal, healthy family. We share a number of rituals, which include annual family vacations and daily dinner together. These help bind us together. We all have own responsibilities to take care of.

"Work is important to me, but my family is my first priority. My kids will only be with me a short time, whereas work will always be there.

"For me and my family, balancing takes a lot of work. My whole idea of balance centers around the spiritual, and our belief in God...covers everything else. One of the ways I keep things in perspective is by asking myself, Am I going to worry about this five years from now? I like to think about the spokes in a wheel to describe my family...there needs to be tension, but if the spokes break or are weakened, then a flat tire results. So we make joint decisions about commitments and responsibilities, all of which are balanced with personal and family needs. Roles are flexible and adaptable, and as the children grow older and more capable, chores change and are often delegated to others.

"I wish I had more time with my husband, but because of work and family, that doesn't happen often.

"It would help if organizations could become more flexible and recognize that families are primary. If not, companies will have increasingly disgruntled employees that will eventually spread like an emotional virus throughout the work force. Managers should become more sensitive to the family needs of their employees and take courses about the realities of family life. There are great needs for daycare, sick care, and support for single parents and blended families.

"Taking time to renew myself helps me to cope with stress, even though family and relationship time are also essential. We try to make memories with one another and occasionally take a 'mad day,' where we will drop out of our normal routine—skip work, skip school—and drive to the redwoods or go to the beach for a sunrise breakfast.

"I think that attitude and remembering why we are here are important for others to consider. I want to be a positive influence on my children, and it's important to me to stay connected to God and to remember that I am en route. It's also important to keep your perspective, to keep your sense of humor, and to remember that you can only do so much. There are times when it is necessary to narrow your scope and focus on just what is right in front of you."

With six children, Chris is aware that she has a limited amount of time and energy for anything else and that balancing is something that must be worked toward continuously. She has both a broad and long-range perspective, which helps her to stay calm amid a very full life. She has made spirituality a central part of her capacity for renewal.

Gary Devlin

Married, two children, with a demanding job that requires extensive travel and time away from home; his wife works closer to home and less than full time

Gary has many of the same struggles that many parents of young children face: having enough time and energy left after work to give the children what they need. Gary, however, has recently set up an office in his home so that he can be close to his kids more easily and more often. I interviewed Gary in his home office, and here is what he has to say:

"There are two metaphors that describe balancing for me. The first is the image of a balance beam where staying on is the main task. If I do too much of one thing, I lose my balance and fall off. To make matters worse, the beam isn't level and it doesn't go in one direction.... How do you stay on when the beam itself is changing?

"My second metaphor has to do with sailing. Sometimes, when going with the wind and the sails are full, life is easier. There are times, though, when you have to go against the wind. At these times, you need more skill; you're more involved in the process of sailing. This symbolizes for me the importance of being conscious of how I live. There are times when I have to reduce the sail area and slow down.... I have to be less grandiose to stay in balance.

"These come together for me in trusting that the movement itself will take me to where I want to go. This means that I have to manage the conflicting demands of children, work, and my relationship with my wife. Whether it is my kids needing me or me needing to be with them, I recognize that underneath any visible tasks, my physical and spiritual well-being serve as a base for those.

"I'm not balancing very well right now. There is too much action in my life to be in balance. But when my life is in balance, I feel light and healthy, like a perfect tack when I'm sailing. When I'm in balance, I may be moving fast, but everything is connected and there is no sense of panic. I'm able to give quality time to all aspects of my life and I feel exhilarated, relaxed, and I just have a ball!

"There are some specific workplace changes that might make balancing easier. We need to redefine success, which begins with a radical reframing of the nature and purpose of business, moving from maximizing profits to creating a sustainable future. When this happens, the infrastructure of organizations will change, particularly in their human resource policies and practices. This includes broadening our view of organizational success from just planning for the next quarter to planning for the next quarter of a century. This would allow us to see the value in taking time off to care for children, because those children will eventually become our customers. As we move toward an information- and service-based economy, our organizations must develop policies that are viable for knowledge workers.

"Because we are in a global economy, learning and learning how to learn are of the utmost importance. Also, it is not as much a matter of learning new things, but remembering. Take time to remember! Our ability to understand and remake our environment has potential for great joy and excitement."

Gary knows what balance feels like and how to move in that direction, but he gets caught up in his work, which he finds engaging. He recognizes the importance of being conscious of his choices and understands that trust and letting go are crucial for being and renewal.

He talked about the importance of remembrance and of moving forward, which for him is part of the spirituality of balancing.

Anita Rios

Married, two young children. Both partners work in demanding, high-pressure jobs

I spoke with Anita in her office and when we were arranging our time to meet, she spoke of the difficulty in balancing her work, family, and personal life. Like many of her contemporaries, she wants to do everything well, and this striving places her under a great deal of stress. Here is what she says:

"Right now in my life, I experience intense pressure, not only to achieve in a workplace that knows no boundaries, but also bringing up a family, caring for aging parents, and contributing to my community. In this country, workaholism is our sanctioned addiction.

"When I think about what balancing looks and feels like, I give thanks first, and have faith that I am put here for a mission, even if I don't know what that is. Every experience is a building block to help prepare me for the next phase.

"If I were to scale back on work, I would put my family at risk. It's important to focus on what is real, not the myths and dreams we perpetuate. By holding on to them, we create pain for ourselves. When all is said and done, I ask myself, How do I want to be remembered? I have my values written on a stack of three-by-five cards and I look at them, and my husband and I talk about them. My top values are personal growth, family, security, health, and my relationship with my husband.

"I would like to see our chief executives and bosses take a look at their own addictions, especially to work. We all need to keep our sense of humor and keep things in perspective. I'd also like to see a blending of all the theories about work into something new and evolving that looks at both micro and macro levels. This new model would focus on how work gets done, with particular emphasis on employees through whom we succeed. What really counts are person-to-person relationships.

"Sometimes I feel like a moth dancing around a flame. I get burned and I learn. Ultimately, that's what I'm here for. Take risks. Learn how to make a difference, to go for it in a smart way."

Anita struggles intensely between creating success and finding meaning. She knows in her heart and mind that there is more to life than achievement, but her needs for perfection often get in the way. This dilemma causes her much pain and stress.

Will Bryce

Married, two young children, both partners in demanding jobs

Will faces enormous pressures that many working couples have to deal with every day. He has a new job, where he feels a need to establish himself, yet he realizes how fast his children are growing and that he might be missing some of the pleasure of watching them grow up. Here are his words:

"Nothing is ever truly in balance for me, but the occasional long weekend spent with my family brings me a great sense of joy. I sacrifice personal time to be with my family and friends, and I don't feel guilty when cutting back at work to be with them. My wife also has a demanding job, and I wonder if I'm doing enough to assist her with the kids. I want to point out how important a satisfactory marriage is to balancing. Being single longer and more settled before marriage has made a big difference.... I can't imagine what it would have been like getting married in my twenties.

"We should take a look at the European model, where they have five to six weeks vacation every year. But it's not going to happen here! Because of the growing trend in changing jobs and careers, employers could help out by offering flexible working hours, as well as supporting childcare programs. I also see that many children are coming of age without proper guidance and that this presents a number of problems we have got to address as a society. Preschool programs, like Head Start, and health care for all children are two specific things we should consider.

"I also wonder how the loss of innocence of our children translates into present and future behaviors. We are undergoing a profound cultural change, and as we assimilate other cultures, we are fast becoming a mosaic, one that is shocking to many. Intolerance of differences, and racism, are major problems, and in many ways we are a large dysfunctional family.... Is it something we can come to grips with?"

Will brings a renewal perspective to balancing as he recognizes that our future rests in our children—his and everyone else's. He has trouble with balancing in his own life, but he does see that time with his children, even if he has to sacrifice some of his own well-being, is of utmost importance. He also recognizes on a larger scale that our society is having difficulty connecting and valuing differences. Will sees that his lack of balance and that of the society as a whole are interconnected.

Ellen Stewart and Roseann Rosetti

Partners, no children, both work full-time and each is considering a job/career change

Ellen and Roseann face most of the same struggles and dilemmas as other couples, but they have the added challenge of being lesbians in a homophobic society. Their words reflect the caring in their relationship. I met with them in their home and here is their story:

Roseann: "Balancing is a challenge for the rest of my life and it is a struggle to monitor the gauges that tell me when I am out of balance. Balancing is continual work and takes focusing and being present."

Ellen: "Balancing has to do with wholeness and my personal quest for that. It is finding a way to honor all those parts of myself."

Roseann: "Scheduling time and knowing what is coming up for each other is also an important part of balancing."

Ellen: "We are explicit about scheduling time together. Sunday is a day just for us."

Roseann: "Also, being twelve years older than Ellen, my career is not as important to me. I'm often a cheerleader for Ellen's career growth."

Ellen: "Balancing doesn't happen often, but it is a sense of groundedness and centeredness."

Roseann: "It is a sense of inner peace, where for brief moments it all clicks together...an inner glow, a feeling of being fed the right diet of mental, physical, and spiritual stimulation. As for our relationship, when we are clicking, we are on a whole other wavelength!"

Ellen: "My individual therapy and our couples therapy helped me to understand and value each other's differences and to communicate more effectively. Therapy has helped us also look at our class differences, our introversion and extroversion, as well as being women in an intimate long-term relationship."

Roseann: "We must value our emotions more, including those who are nurturers and caretakers."

Ellen: "Work is an issue of godliness in this culture to the point that things not-work are a sin. Our buzzwords of the month, like 'do more with less,' 'lean and mean,' and so on, though they often lead to burnout, are not seen as a problem in this society."

Roseann: "Play is part of balance. We don't really know how to play. We lost our ability to do something that is just fun, because 'if you have fun, you're not being productive.' What does that three letter word [fun] mean, anyway?"

Ellen: "What's valued in our society? Heart or nonheart? Helpers, especially, need to understand the conflict of someone who wants to be whole in a society and workplace that says be only part of who you are or cut off part of yourself. How can we flourish, given that reality?"

Ellen and Roseann are aware of many of society's shadow characteristics, and they realize that this makes balancing a real struggle in their lives and work. Their relationship is a central part of their balancing process, and they are willing to seek therapy and help when this is too difficult. They also recognize the power of balancing as a beacon providing light and energy to their lives each day. For them, continuing to connect and communicate with one another, even if difficult or awkward, is important to their relationship and in moving toward balance in their lives.

Jack Chaynor and Karen Davies

Married, three teenage children, Jack is an entrepreneur, and Karen works part-time, having recently gone through a major career transition

I interviewed Jack and Karen separately. They were both open and engaging, and in many ways have worked through a number of the issues that the other couples and families are still struggling with. For convenience, I've woven their interviews together.

Jack: "My first priority is my family, but as an entrepreneur, it is easy to end up working all the time. In earlier days, when setting my goals, I would put more attention on the work side, and when I achieved those, I found it wasn't what I wanted. Recently, I have begun putting family at the center when I set my goals, and interestingly enough, the work takes care of itself. As a result, I have a pretty healthy family life. But I have to pay attention to make it happen."

Karen: "My reaction to balancing is, 'Oh, boy!' I love my work and my family, and I now feel that developing in both areas has made me a better mother. I feel I've given my children the gift of autonomy. But during that time, I felt like I was flying. The harder I worked, the more I took on and the more energy I had. But as I wound down that period of my life, I went into a collapse that was marked by depression and got sick quite often. When I'm in balance, I feel calmer about things. There is also lots of laughter!"

Jack: "Karen and I schedule regular time together. One of the things we do is take country and western dancing lessons. I attend personal growth classes and even got my son to go with me one time. I also play games with my kids.

"As for what would make balancing easier, first of all, deficit spending destroys the earning power of the average citizen and is the biggest destroyer of family life. Since television is insidious and like a magnet for free time and energy, I recommend we destroy our TV sets. Since fatigue is a real problem for so many people, I would require everyone to take a two-hour nap every afternoon! One other thought: I would lock families in a room for a few hours and force them to talk to one another."

Karen: "Balancing won't happen through macro-level changes, but it will occur through individuals being in pain and honestly telling their stories to each other. Society will change when enough individuals begin to change. Get rid of advertising in all forms! Make nature available to people. Get out of the city and experience silence. Build communities; stay connected with nature. We must lower taxes because they are so arbitrary and people have no real control over them."

Jack: "I had to go through a number of ups and downs to learn the lessons I now know. It's important to trust your own experience. It's also imperative that we let go of this huge attention we have toward business and work."

Karen: "It's important to find time to be alone and in solitude. Each of us is our own best guide. Be patient with yourself, choose partners and friends wisely. Today's balance may not work tomorrow…be flexible.

"It reminds me of a performance of a Chinese acrobatic troupe I saw several years ago. There were several chairs that were stacked on top of one another in all sorts of angles, which formed a swaying, balanced sculpture upon which sat one of the acrobats. It was almost a living thing…there was movement and a lot of self-correction in it…. I recognized that it is okay to fail or fall, and that if I cling to balance, I've already lost it. Balance is not about perfection. Instead, it's about swaying."

Both Jack and Karen brought a light and open attitude to their interviews, both laughing easily. Jack acknowledged how difficult balancing is and how much care and attention is required. Karen understands that balancing is a process and the work required basically never ends. But rather than seeing this as burdensome, both of them realize that the tension, the "swaying," is what balancing is all about.

Alan Feld and Gary Lassen

Partners, no children, Alan works part-time and Gary consults, having just left a full-time corporate position

Gary and Alan are a couple deeply committed to one another. They face most of the same issues as any other couple as well as the added issue of HIV. Here is their interview:

Gary: "Balancing has to do with values and the struggle of what it means to be at work with its endless demands."

Alan: "I don't let work overwhelm me. Work is circumscribed and rarely spills over into my home life. I have other responsibilities, including an active volunteer life, that I value as much as my work. I make lists for everything, but I take a philosophical view and ask myself,

What is the worst thing if it doesn't get done? Work is a tyrant in Gary's life!"

Gary: "Volunteerism is something I value, too, because it's something I want to do and it feeds more back into me."

Alan: "We are both HIV positive, and I feel a double bind of feeling a sense of pressure to get everything done versus not overstressing my system. The ideas of fun and relaxation have a hard time making themselves heard."

Gary: "I need to be pragmatic about this…concerned for medical benefits. I'm considering a career in consulting, but the question of 'What happens if I get sick?' plays a big part in my decision. There is also the issue of becoming caretakers for friends and the specter of dealing with so many people who are getting sick and dying…. I use work as a way to get away from HIV, HIV, HIV!"

Alan: "My grief and low-grade depression impact those areas that could bring joy and relief, most notably our sexual activity. We do take joy from our work, go on vacations together, and we have created little sillinesses that give us respite and space to move into another world."

Gary: "When I'm in balance, I feel peaceful and serene. Things just go right. I focus inward, I'm satisfied, physically calmer, and energy is just there. I am more open and able to be a part of what is going on around me. Love and spirit are a big part of balance for me."

Alan: "I experience a sense of relaxation and I don't feel the pressure of the demands in my life. For me, taking the time to lay out in the sun is the best way to be in balance. It entails putting myself in a place where I can fall asleep."

Gary: "I think flextime and job sharing are needed in organizations, whether this is to take care of children, sick friends, or aging parents. I believe there should be respect given to our other obligations and that employees shouldn't have to continually make either/or choices."

Alan: "Daycare, reduced hours, and part-time employment would also be important. We have high unemployment at the same time that many people are working longer and longer hours. There must be some way to balance this."

Gary: "Many people have increasingly long commutes, which, if in a car, can be frustrating, stressful, and unproductive. We should think about reshaping work, where people could work at home a good part of the time."

Alan: "With too few people doing too much work, it creates stress for everyone. Two-career families are devastating for kids! Where children are raised without nurturing, what will they be like when they grow up…? Set limits. Learn how to say no. Validate yourself for what you do and do not put yourself down for what you don't do."

Gary: "People need to look inside and become aware of their values. The question becomes, How much are you willing to give up to get what you want? Parents should take some of the pressure off their kids so they don't have to grow up being so frenetic."

Alan: "Don't catastrophize everything. There are very few true life-and-death situations!"

As Alan's last words indicate, he and Gary bring a sense of perspective to their lives that most of us find difficult to achieve. They obviously face a number of issues that make balancing problematic, but they do see it is important in their lives. Gary knows the importance of looking at his values, but he struggles to keep work in its place. This affects Alan and their relationship. Together, they recognize the necessity of being with children and teaching them that there is more to life than success and accomplishment.

Dana Mangioni

Married, two small children, very ambitious and career-focused, husband currently at home with children

Dana is dedicated to both her career and her family. Dana's story is unlike any others in this book, and somewhat unusual in our society. Listen to what she says:

"My husband is a full-time 'Mr. Mom,' and our kids have never seen their dad wear a tie. They occasionally ask, 'Why do only mommies work?' The word that comes to me about balancing is *imperfection*. I am never in balance, but rather than being tough on myself, I prefer to redefine what balance is and then to manage my expectations accordingly. There are definitely peaks and valleys, and because I travel frequently, I often don't see the kids for long periods of time. I have learned to laugh at myself and to keep things in perspective.

"What am I doing, working the long hours, being the single income for my family, is seen as bizarre by some of my co-workers. I am proud to be a spectacle! There is, though, the implication that something is wrong with our family. I often get asked, 'When will your husband get a job?' or 'Can't you relocate?' My response is to educate others by telling them how my husband and I planned and prepared for this, how we made a conscious choice together, how well it's working, and how happy we both are! I am very explicit in reminding others that this is our choice; I wouldn't be happy at home, nor would my husband be happy in an office.

"I see a time coming when managers are more open-minded regarding work and family. Senior managers must develop a greater comfort level with these issues and concerns, and balancing will become easier as more women with balance in their lives reach higher levels in their organizations. I would also like not to be second-guessed about my capabilities and hope the assumptions that women are not as flexible and dedicated to their work will begin to change.

"On a different track, I feel that the high cost of living prohibits many from taking the risks to seek out new and appropriate options. We need also to accept that men are capable as nurturers and childcare providers.

"Getting your dream doesn't come by wishing and hoping. A lot of hard work is necessary and the process is not always logical and you will be on your own much of the way. But you are surrounded and in good company. Talk about it and you'll find others feeling exactly the same way."

Dana is living and working under a new paradigm, one that she and her husband have created together, to meet their individual and family needs. They are breaking the rules and questioning some of our most tightly held assumptions about work and sex roles. Dana and her husband are truly creating their own way of balancing.

For these these couples and families, there is a strong commitment to self and family, but it looks as though many are unable or unwilling to let go of their strong achievement needs, in spite of their need toward the importance of balancing, taking time to do nothing, or being with their partners and children. The pressures from their workplaces, and a culture that so highly values doing, combine to counteract what these interviewees know intellectually and intuitively: that there is more, much more, to life than work.

Issues and Challenges Faced by Couples and Families

1. It is a struggle finding the time and having the skills for quality communication, especially of an intimate nature.
2. There is an impermanence in relationships of all kinds, making it difficult for people to feel a sense of community and belonging.
3. The many newer forms of families are often not fully accepted or understood by others.
4. With rules and roles blurred and changing, partners often find it confusing and difficult to get their needs met.
5. There is the ongoing dilemma of personal identity aligned with couple/family identity.
6. There is difficulty integrating values from different families of origin.
7. It is difficult finding time for self, especially for women in traditional male/female relationships.
8. It is hard dealing with a slow-to-change or an inflexible workplace, especially when childcare and flexible scheduling are a concern.
9. The need for perfection or trying to do it all can cause problems.
10. Many feel sandwiched between their children and aging parents.

Strategies for Working Through the Issues and Challenges   89

1. Learn and practice positive communicating and negotiating skills.
2. Schedule time together, including family vacations or time away from it all.
3. Learn and practice joint decision making, including the children as they become old enough to participate.
4. Delegate chores, and if affordable, pay others to do those for which you have no time.
5. Give up on stereotyped or old notions of what a family should be like. Instead, create your own definitions of what this is and don't let judgments of others deter you from living that way.
6. Throttle back on your career and work, if possible, and let go of having to climb to the top of whatever pyramid you've planted in your mind.
7. Negotiate with your workplaces for more flexibility, both for you and co-workers, now and in the future.
8. Read and ponder meaningful books, inspiring art, music, and poetry, together.
9. Try couple and family therapy, not just when you are in crisis or overwhelmed, but also as an ongoing growth process.
10. See your life, work, and family as whole and life affirming, and not as separate pieces of a pie.

8

Balancing in the Workplace

It would be possible to write an entire book about workplaces and balance, and in fact many of the current popular business books focus on how to harness and nurture the hearts and minds of employees. These books speak about learning, creativity, and flexibility and point out both theoretically and anecdotally what virtually everyone who has ever had a job knows and what I've heard time and again from employees and career counseling clients: "When I feel good about my workplace, when I am supported, trusted, and given the tools to do a job I am interested in, I will perform admirably. On the other hand, if you do not trust me, or you deceive me or abuse me, no matter what good reasons you have for doing so, you will never really have my full attention and energy. If you want me to be effective in my work, you have to demonstrate consistent concern for my well-being."

This chapter will weave a number of interviews together with observations, knowledge, and comments I have picked up over the past several years doing seminars and workshops on balancing in the workplace. The interviews offer a number of differing viewpoints and attitudes, not all of which support the concept of balancing I have presented in this book. In my seminars, I also experienced many different attitudes about balancing in the workplace, some feeling that this is "The Answer," others quite hostile to the idea, and still others fearful of what it might mean if they were to move their organizations in this direction or if they themselves were to ask their organizations to be more responsive to employees' needs for greater balance.

I often get asked in my presentations if there is such a thing as a balancing organization or if I have seen a movement in that direction. What I have seen are many managers and decision makers, as well as many others on their way to the top levels in their organizations, who embrace the idea that employee well-being and organizational effectiveness are inexorably linked, two sides of the same coin. For a number of years, many organizations have put the importance of their human resources, their people, on a pedestal. The hard reality, however, as employees know, is that often the touted attention to employee needs is a myth and one all too often perceived as a cruel hoax. Those organizations in which employees are the most cynical, angry, and frustrated are those in which the gap between the professed value of people and the actual human resource practices are the widest.

A balancing organization does not necessarily value people more than profits, but rather develops attitudes, practices, and internal competencies that allow it to flexibly honor both. In a world where many managers and business owners have lived and died by either/or thinking, holding to a both/and view of their business is a challenge of monumental proportions. Many leaders give lip service to these newer ideas, but in the heat of the battle, they often slide back into older, easier patterns of behavior. The balancing organization will find unique and creative ways to integrate both ends of the paradox, and such places will become the excellent workplaces of the twenty-first century.

Before getting into the interviews, I'd like to share two illustrations of the push and pull in our workplaces during this time of transition. One comes from a recent advertisement from IBM. It is titled, interestingly enough, "Balancing Act," and shows a picture of a father, obviously working at home, with his young daughter being given a piggyback ride, even as he works at his computer. Both father and daughter are smiling. Subtitled "The first computer to understand you don't just have a job. You have a life," the copy reads, "Something fundamental has changed in America. Now it's not just the living you make, it's the life you make. You want to enjoy the things you're supposedly working for. Your family. Your home. Yourself." This marvelous ad goes on to detail how the quality of your computer can improve the quality of your life, and concludes with: "You may need more than just a perfectly balanced computer to find your own perfect balance. But who knows? You might just do your best work with someone looking over your shoulder."[7]

This ad illustrates a number of significant workplace changes. First of all is the explicit acknowledgment that balancing is becoming increasingly important for people. Second, it highlights a growing trend of people working at home and the technology that makes this possible. It also implicitly recognizes that fathers are wanting to be more involved in nurturing and parenting. All this adds up, in a single, well-crafted advertisement, to a succinct illustration of how our workplaces have changed so dramatically.

The second is a story I heard during one of my interviews and shows the opposite end of the spectrum regarding work in the 1990s. Some may question whether this story is true, but most who have worked in a corporation will understand its point. It seems that an overweight female employee became pregnant. As her pregnancy progressed, she was able to hide this fact at her workplace. She did not tell her boss or her co-workers for fear of losing her job, or at least being questioned about her plans after the baby was born. So she shared her pregnancy with no one at work.

Months later, her baby was born on a Friday, with mother and daughter both healthy. The following Monday morning, she called in to work saying she needed the week off to attend to some family business. No further explanation was asked for or given. The next Monday, ten days after having a baby, she was back at work. No one knew she had been pregnant. No one knew she had just had a baby. She again told no one and simply went back to work as usual.

This story and the computer ad together indicate the chaos and uncertainty, the range of ambiguity, that accompanies the changes going on in our workplaces. Some companies are moving forward adeptly, recognizing that the hearts, hands, and minds of their employees are needed to weather the storm of this transition period. Others are reluctant, even resistant, and may need to be dragged kicking and screaming into the future, or they may vanish from the scene altogether, much as the dinosaurs did many millions of years ago.

The difficulties and struggles faced by our workplaces are huge, and from what I have observed, even the most capable and farsighted are struggling to make sense of their environment. They are often torn between many dilemmas: cutting costs and managing for today versus planning for the longer term; getting their goods and services to customers quickly versus the training and development needs of their employees; enhancing efficiency throughout the organization versus human resistance to changing so much and so fast. Amid all this turmoil, it should be no surprise that our workplaces are hungry for answers for success and survival in a changed and changing world.

Simon Trevino

Chief technology officer for a computer manufacturer

Simon represents the technological side, which is becoming a more crucial part of every workplace. He struggles with the dilemma of productivity of his employees versus a culture and system in which long hours and workaholic behaviors are the norm. Here is what Simon has to say:

"Many of my employees are classic workaholics, who are often working so hard, they don't know when they're becoming less effective. They tend to see every problem or crisis as equal, and their need for perfection makes it difficult for them to see alternative solutions or to see their work in any other way. Consequently, these employees can be difficult to manage and counsel. Furthermore, the idea of 'zero defects,' which I understand as a process, is seen by many of my employees as an absolute.

"For the first time, however, my organization and I are challenging this workaholism, to the point of forcing employees to take vacation, who are often resentful at having to take time away from their jobs. I also realize that working harder is not necessarily the answer, and I am working to design the business process so that people can be successful in forty hours a week. This 'working smarter' is hard to instill in others, because it must be taught by example. To this end, I've begun to delegate more of the technical decisions to my reports, as well as continually asking myself, What piece of information do I have that others need to come to the right decision?

"About a year and a half ago I had a major heart attack, and when I returned to work several months later, I worked just four hours a day. I restructured my job so that I could get it done part-time, and found myself surprised that I was able to accomplish so much in so little time. I am now back to working full-time, but I'm clear I do not want to work the way I used to before the attack. In fact, I am more productive now and am one of the most accessible vice presidents in the company.

"On a personal level, I feel less stressed. Before my heart attack, there was no time to wind down. I am more in tune with my energy level, and when I'm tired, whether mentally or physically, I take walks and try to make no decisions of any importance. I also do not take as much work home from the office as I did before. Even before the heart attack, I was predisposed to do things differently, but, I might add, I wouldn't be as far along. My wife occasionally has to remind me, 'You can play even if there are things that have to be done.'

"My first bit of advice having to do with balance begins with spending time figuring out how things are changing both inside and outside the company and asking, 'Why are we moving this way?' To this I would add that it is important to ask not only 'How should we do things better?' but also asking 'Why should we be doing this in the first place?' So for me and my employees, the 'what' we do, the quality of things, is of utmost importance. It is critical to step back long enough and far enough to get perspective on what is really happening. Finally, I'd like to say that everything is temporary, including you. Let go. People who are slaves to their jobs aren't in control."

96   Simon is a progressive manager, but I wonder how many others out there will wait until a heart attack or other crisis before they recognize that long hours and workaholic behavior are not the answers. Simon also has a larger and more long-term perspective than many of his counterparts. His challenge will be to sustain this knowledge and understanding in light of the competitive pressures that his organization will inevitably face.

At one high-technology firm where I have done several presentations on balancing work and personal life, many of the questions and concerns reflect the anxiety and overwhelming effect of working long hours and not feeling that you can say no to workplace demands. At the end of one of the sessions, a question from the back of the room was, "Shouldn't you be telling all this stuff to our chief executive officer?" There was much laughter and heads nodding in agreement. After some thought, I answered this way: "Yes, I should, but realistically, I don't think I will get the opportunity to tell him these things. First of all, from his vantage point, he feels little of the pain and frustration you experience. You all work very hard to make this company successful, and that is what is of prime concern to him. As long as you continue to do this, he has little incentive to see and do things differently. Second, even if he did invite me to speak with him, I don't believe he would hear the messages in the same way you do. He makes a lot of money and has enough power to insulate himself from the daily travails that make your lives difficult. So he has no perceived need to hear me. However, if you can get me an invitation, I will certainly speak with him!"

This story comes out of a well-respected, fast growing manufacturing firm and I tell it to illustrate the gap in understanding and behavior between employees' wants and needs and those of the decision makers. Many employees make the connection that they are more productive and creative when in balance, but as long as they continue to work the long and hard hours, even if it leads to burnout and stress, organizational leaders have little incentive to do things differently. When employees begin to say no, sometimes at tremendous risk to their careers, then and only then will organizational decision makers have real reason to hear these issues.

Alicia Hamilton

Senior vice president and chief operating officer at her current company

Alicia has held several senior level positions in her career, and her interview reflected a broad perspective on balancing. She believes that how you treat your people, no matter what business you are in, is a defining characteristic of successful organizations. Here are Alicia's words:

"Enlightened management gets more productivity! I want to emphasize that by investing in our people, whether through training, morale-building events, and so on, you create a positive team atmosphere. By recognizing employees as people, you can get a lot more from them.

"I recognize that budgetary constraints are real, but I always ask, 'How long does it take to recognize employees?' Yes, good training is expensive and takes people off the job while they are in training. But there is a huge cost in turnover that is often the result of poor management, and this cost, the loss of productivity, is often not recognized by managers. The biggest handicap for management people is that they do not know how to give honest, constructive feedback. Because we are afraid to tell the truth, employees never change.

"If organizations examined the costs and benefits of training and other human resource programs, it would not be difficult to make a business case for these programs. If costs are a concern, my suggestion is to find the person inside the company who is the best in a particular area and have them train others. Relying on in-house expertise this way cuts costs and builds morale at the same time. When people are happier, they are more productive.

"Developing better communication skills between people would make balancing easier. This should begin in high schools, and perhaps even as early as elementary school. I also believe that self-esteem training should be incorporated into our lives, and that we need to recognize each other's worth and positively communicate that to one another. Furthermore, I suggest that counseling and therapy be available to everyone.

"It's important to keep one's sense of humor. Also, we have to care about the people we work with, and for managers in particular, the people who work for you. If you're unhappy, find out why. Be proactive in your own life."

Alicia sees that communication and trust, characteristics of finding meaning, have a direct and measurable impact on the bottom line. She is also very open to some of the so-called "softer" sides of employee needs and concerns, that people's feelings and their self-esteem are not only personal issues, but also impact how they perform in their jobs.

Recently, I did a half-day seminar for a group of independent consultants who provide communication and public relations services to large and small businesses. Many of these people were motivated to start and run their own businesses because they were looking for a better balance between work and their personal and family lives. What most had found, however, is that working for oneself is rarely the ticket to more freedom and greater balance. On the contrary, although most of these people loved their work and being their own boss, they found it extremely difficult to achieve any real sense of balance in their lives.

As an exercise, I asked them to recall a time in their lives when they experienced balance and then asked them to describe what that looked and felt like. Though a few described their current situations as a source of balance, most had to go back into their past, and one person recalled sadly that the last time he remembered feeling balance was many years before as a child living on a farm. The ensuing discussion about the gap between their needs for balance and the reality of their independent way of making a living helped many realize that they had no more balance working on their own than they had as employees.

The remainder of the seminar was devoted to articulating the sources of imbalance, which for most was a variation of too much time working and not enough time to enjoy the fruits of their labor. However, as they began to identify the various discrepancies between what they wanted and how they actually worked and lived, many came to recognize that they had been repeating the same work-oriented pattern they were living when they were employees. As they developed specific plans to achieve a better balance in their work, family, and personal lives, the most typical solution had to do with saying no and setting firm limits on their work in order to have time and energy for those other important parts of their lives.

Tom Del Vecchio

Manages the West Coast branch of a laboratory that provides scientific testing to the biotechnology industry

Though Tom's organization is small, employing about thirty people, he sees the same issues as those faced in Fortune 500 companies. But because he can be involved in all phases of the business, he knows his people well, and his hands-on style mitigates some of the more pressing challenges. Here is what he has to say:

"Many of my employees struggle with setting boundaries, especially between work and home. This is particularly true of my managers, who are more prone to burnout, which I believe results when people are not able to set these boundaries. I wonder how I should intervene in someone's life when I see them struggling, and I recognize that there is a fine line between probing too far into one's nonwork life and letting people work things out for themselves.

"In thinking about changes that would make balancing easier, I have begun to use a bonus structure that is based not only on 'stretch goals' but also on less quantifiable things like staff development, service level improvements, and so on. There is then a quarterly review, based on their goals, and a self-review. This process gives employees a sense of control over their own performance and gets their level of thinking and consciousness above the day-to-day din. I'm also moving toward clarifying responsibilities and priorities for all employees by developing meaningful, yet flexible job descriptions. I believe that meeting agendas can serve as progress reports as well as being used to set priorities and make decisions about how and where to allocate one's time. New agendas show items completed from previous weeks so that people obtain a sense of progress.

"I also think that we should recognize the reality of human error and frailty, even though standards and expectations remain high. Similarly, we should look at the context and accept limitations, including those

100   imposed by the marketplace. Give recognition for past performance, and emphasize the value of the process over the results. We need to remember that all change is incremental and that accountability helps structure boundaries and liberates you from being accountable outside those boundaries.

"Finally, I believe there is a spiritual side to this process. Many people are experiencing a spiritual malaise, and we need to deal with this to create a healthier workplace. This may not be a widely acknowledged view, but I think it's important to look at these deeper and longer-range issues and concerns."

Tom embodies much of the spirit of generative balancing, especially in his closing comments. Tom recognizes that a critical component of balancing, and ultimately productivity, is learning how to set and live with boundaries, which is part of connecting with one another.

A well-known and highly respected technology manufacturer is looking at ways to balance its work force, even going so far as having created a position to guide the organization in this effort. In theory, this process and person will look at the changing needs inside the company over time and design methods to rebalance the mix of skills and jobs to the tasks needing to be done as the organization moves into the future.

In the short term, however, the reality has been different. This organization has a history of not laying off employees, and instead it is redeploying people, giving them the opportunity to find new jobs within the company in a time frame of several months. If they find nothing during this time, they must then either take any job that is currently available, even if their skills are not a match, or take the severance package and leave.

While this process may eventually have a positive impact on building a more effective organization, there are numerous stories from managers about being forced to hire employees even when there is no apparent need or taking on others whose skills do not match the needs of their business. This organization is caught between short-term competitive pressures and its culture of taking care of its employees over the long term. Their efforts at work force balancing are on the right track and should eventually pay huge dividends, if they can manage to keep their attention focused on the mutual goals of organizational effectiveness and employee well-being.

Gwen Quant

Head of human resources for a large food retailer

Gwen sees that the traditional ways of doing business are no longer adequate in our competitive economy. She is working toward influencing her organization to be more flexible and innovative and faces a number of struggles as a result. Here is her story:

"There is a real need for my organization to look at new and nontraditional ways of how work gets done. I would like to see an environment where this organization is seen as the employer of choice. My company needs to offer reasons for people to come work here, and I see that cultural diversity and issues for women will become increasingly important. At the same time, however, I also see tough times ahead for my industry and company. Job security as a driving force is an increasingly artificial concept.

"We are looking at the ways jobs are done and exploring the notions of doing work at home one day a week, job sharing, and have begun testing the idea of co-managers for some of our stores. Keeping women in the pipeline is difficult.... We are losing them to child rearing, and if we don't do some of these more innovative things, we won't be able to stay competitive. The problem for me, though, is that as I challenge the status quo, I run the risk of being viewed as a troublemaker.

"There are a number of difficulties in doing these new things, however. Being in retail, scheduling is always an issue, because to do the job, you have to be in the store. Job sharing, though, is one answer to this dilemma. Our union contracts, which are seniority-driven, dictate schedules, making flexibility even more difficult. My company has abdicated responsibility for employees to the union, and there is a lack of cooperation and ongoing conflicts between the company and the union.

"My advice to others begins with establishing how the things you propose to help employees will also help the company. Figure out ways to show how these proposals are good for the organization, including benchmarking to other companies and getting ideas from others. You have to start by involving your people and finding out what they really want and need. And don't get locked into one way of seeing or doing things. Be flexible to changes in the environment."

If there is a word that captures Gwen's attitude in her work, that would be *flexibility*. That she sees this as crucial to the navigating needs of her company is testament both to her foresight and willingness to risk in order to see her organization be successful. She also understands the importance of connecting, both on issues of diversity in considering nontraditional ways of recruiting, retaining, and developing employees.

Not long ago I did a presentation to a group of mid- and senior-level human resource professionals from a variety of organizations, mostly high-technology manufacturing firms. As I described generative balancing to them, several consistent concerns surfaced. The first had to with questions of implementation. The managers wondered about how they would train their people to balance. They also asked, "How do we build the ideas, questions, attitudes, and skills into our existing training programs?" and "How do we sell our chief executives and other line managers on this amorphous and hard-to-quantify notion of balance?" and "What exactly is the connection between balancing and the bottom line?"

Many of these legitimate concerns came out of a healthy skepticism and natural wariness of a new idea. I certainly could understand that. However, underneath many of the questions and comments was fear, a fear that centered on the implicit question of, How do I put these ideas out to my organization without putting myself at risk? Though there was much interest, I realized that not everyone is ready or willing to take the risks implied in moving toward a balancing organization.

Glynn Harris

Chief operating officer for a manufacturing firm

Glynn heads a successful company, one considered a leader both in products and its progressive management and human resource practices. As you will soon see, however, he takes a more traditional view on the relationship between the organization and its employees. Here is what he has to say:

"There are requirements of the workplace and home life. I believe that home should take precedence, but sometimes it doesn't. I don't know if imbalance impacts productivity, but as I think about it, tugging from home does intervene in work productivity. If an employee's personal life is detracting from their work, I am willing to give them time off to fix or improve the situation. On a personal level, because my wife and I have no children, I have a relatively easy time balancing.

"My advice to others is that it is important for people to be as productive as possible at work, so that they can have time for their family. I suggest that people be disciplined and organized and to be tough on themselves and just get it done! Also, compare your schedule to what you actually get done, and you'll probably see a lot of wasted time. I have been beating a drum called 'cycle time,' or how long it takes to get things done, which can be continually sped up by eliminating or minimizing downtime. The key to thinking about this is being conscious."

Glynn was all business in our interview and it was clear that he has a different perspective on balancing than I do. His story is a clear reminder that there are numerous ways to think about balancing and probably as many ways to move successfully into the future. He reminds us of the importance of being conscious as we move forward in our work and lives.

In a presentation on generative balancing for a staff of internal career development specialists, the specialists raised a number of comments and questions that I consider worth sharing:

- "When people take time for themselves, they don't know what to do."

- "Do you see that with the changes in organizations [restructuring and downsizing] that it is becoming tougher to balance?"
- "Do I give up 'having enough' to get more of my spiritual needs met?"
- "Is a big part of balancing simply letting go?"
- "Getting people to examine themselves in a downsizing organization is very difficult."
- "This [balancing] is countercultural in a sense, because in many organizations the idea is to keep others off balance. You're saying it might be good to turn this around."
- "I wonder how high up this will be accepted in an organization, if they [senior-level managers] even understand it?"
- "Do people ever acknowledge that money and power are what lead to imbalance?"
- "This [generative balancing] could become a requirement for the Baldridge [Quality] Award. Then you would see corporations getting it out there."
- "If I'm imbalanced, what values am I teaching my children?"
- "If enough individuals start using something like this, even for themselves, then it will be felt in the organization."
- "The real truth. You will make sacrifices...it will cost you something."
- "How do we renew ourselves daily so we don't feel the need for drastic steps?"

Another recent presentation was made to a group of one hundred professionals and managers who were currently out of work. As I prepared to talk to them about balancing, I was at first hesitant and anxious. I felt that their immediate needs of finding work and getting reemployed would far outweigh the notion of balancing.

As they began to question and challenge me, my anxiety disappeared. Though unemployed—and many obviously depressed and discouraged—they raised issues that were less about creating success and more about finding meaning and renewing themselves. I began to see that though they had some immediate needs and real concerns, many were using at least some of this time to ponder some of these deeper and more subtle issues. Many of their questions, and especially some of their comments during the presentation and afterward, were focused on gaining a larger perspective in their lives and recognizing that as important as work was to them, they realized—some for the first time—how much more there is to their lives.

Rose Fiondisalla

Head of human resources for a start-up high-technology company

Rose is acutely aware of the need for balancing, both as a productivity issue and as a personal need and value. In fact, she left a high-visibility senior-level human resources job recently because of the demands and now works three days a week in her current position. Rose has this to say:

"I believe that an organization has the responsibility to provide motivating work and the employee the responsibility to balance their lives. In my organization, software engineers work a lot because they love the work, but the company can send the message that balance is important. This is done primarily from the value set projected by the leaders of the organization.

"There are times when the organization needs more productivity than employees can give. Employees, in turn, must decide when to say no, and then comes the issue of how that is received by the organization. The organization must also wrestle with the ongoing dilemma of needing employees to be available versus wanting them to be so. This necessitates knowing and setting boundaries, but also being able to cross over them as necessary.

"In fact, the entire software group telecommutes two days a week. This is for retention purposes and is used to recruit new talent as well. I believe in being very honest with employees and asking them to 'Decide if this is the right environment for you.' There is often exaggeration about the long hours many employees proudly proclaim, and the real problem is not so much the long hours but that work gets into your system and you can't get it out—and this is what takes the real

106   toll. The social norm of work is so strong that I used to feel guilty leaving at six or seven P.M., even after putting in a full, productive day!

"Balance is different for everyone and the company should not legislate it. If your most valued employee said, 'I can't take this!,' then what would you be willing to do to keep that person? The biggest fallacy in many organizational leaders' minds is, What if everyone wanted to do this? I also want to make it clear that it is okay to ask people to make trade-offs to get the flexibility they may want and need.

"One more thing is that we often underestimate the power of technology in dealing with issues of balance. Its power, however, cuts both ways. When the computer is on and is everywhere, you can potentially work twenty-four hours a day. At the same time, however, you can work virtually anywhere and don't always—or ever, in some cases—have to be on site. Technology can be a huge part of the solution. But it can also follow you home."

Rose's interview is purposely the last one in this chapter. She clearly describes the dilemmas inherent in balancing, both from an organizational perspective and from an individual point of view. She recognizes that balancing is an ongoing process and that it is an emerging recruitment and retention tool. As her comments illustrate, balancing presents organizations with a number of cultural and logistical problems.

These interviews and stories show many perspectives on balancing, and they by no means cover the entire spectrum. That there is growing awareness and recognition of the need for balance is seen in support for childcare and flexible scheduling that is shown in many organizations today. Generative balancing has much appeal to organizations, but at the same time, it forces them to face a number of dilemmas that in the short term often seem best left unaddressed. As many of the interviews and anecdotes illustrated, workplaces, just as with individuals and families, have needs that are not being met under the old models. Generative balancing won't provide all the answers, but it can offer a way for organizations and workplaces to respond expansively and embrace a new paradigm, which is perhaps the real task of leadership for the twenty-first century.

There is another way to think about how generative balancing applies to organizations. The creating success competency has to do with managing in organizations those tasks and issues necessary to keep an enterprise successfully engaged in the world. Finding meaning lies within the realm of leadership and appears lacking in all but the very best organizations. It will require the commitment of the leaders and the employees to weave this competency into the plans and tasks that lead to true greatness. Organizational renewal can be likened to stewardship, which has to do with guiding businesses in such a way as to enhance the lives of anyone or anything that will be touched by its efforts. If those of us in organizations can see that management, leadership, and stewardship are all vital pieces of the puzzle, we will find that there will be greater balance in our lives and work.

Issues and Challenges Faced by Workplaces

1. Numerous and complex dilemmas come up with greater frequency in a global and rapidly changing economy.
2. Communication, especially negative feedback, in all directions is often unclear, poorly timed, and not honest.
3. There is not enough or the right kind of training.
4. Employees are under increasing pressure and stress from growing workloads and continuing off-work responsibilities.
5. Employees and bosses often cannot or will not set boundaries between work and nonwork.
6. Many people experience malaise, fatigue, stress, or a feeling of being overwhelmed at the same time that workplaces need the full energy and attention of everyone.
7. Such issues as diversity and new definitions of success present workplaces with complexities for which there are few models to guide them.

108

8. There is a need to remake or redesign workplaces, not just in reaction to a crisis, but to build adaptable and resilient organizations.

9. The need to recruit and retain the best talent becomes a crucial component of competitive advantage as we move more into a service- and information-oriented economy.

Strategies for Working Through the Issues and Challenges

1. Managers and leaders must begin to look at their businesses in longer time frames and broader perspectives.

2. Teach everyone in the organization how to give and receive feedback, not just at performance appraisal time, but as an integral part of doing business.

3. Evaluate training needs thoroughly for present and future competencies. Design innovative and flexible training programs that are portable, accessible, and easily adaptable. Evaluate training programs and their effectiveness over longer time horizons.

4. Move toward flexibility in such areas as scheduling, where people work, how they dress, and compensation and reward systems. Make sure that these new arrangements are valued in the same ways as the more traditional arrangements.

5. Health benefits should begin to be built on the concept of wellness, with employee assistance and mental health as an integral part of those programs.

6. Policies, procedures, and the culture itself should deemphasize workaholism and long hours as badges of honor and instead should support vacations and other types of leave as signs of working smarter.

7. Performance appraisals should be realistic and honest and should value both qualitative and quantitative measures. There should be several sources of input; appraisals should measure such qualities as willingness to take risks, continuous learning, and creative problem solving.

8. Question your most sacred assumptions about your organization and where it is going. The generative balancing questions, for example, can be a part of an annual organization-wide strategic planning process.

9. Encourage and reward skill acquisition and continuous learning, even if these will not be used until some time in the future. Create opportunities for training wherever possible, for both trainers and trainees.

10. Develop mechanisms and systems to identify emerging skills and competencies, both those that will be needed and those that the organization currently has. Create processes to assess the gaps and build in to the organization ways to close the gaps.

Time Out for Balancing

This time-out is similar to the first, except that it is more a stream of consciousness, uninterrupted by the periodic questioning of the earlier one. I encourage you to take whatever time you need to experience your feelings, moving slowly and calmly through the process. You may, again, want to record your responses and feelings in a journal or diary.

Imagine that you are leaving a theater, where you have just seen one of the most moving and inspiring productions you have ever witnessed…. As you step out of the theater, you are instantly transported to a time and place where you feel peace and wholeness. You may have been there before, or perhaps this is a place you have imagined or dreamed about. It is your place—where you feel calm and complete….

As you meander slowly through your scene, the thoughts and feelings that come to you are ones of being okay with yourself and the world. Work, worries, anxieties are no longer issues for you, not necessarily because you've resolved your questions, but for this time and in this place, the questions, however pressing or worrisome, are of no consequence to you….

You continue to stroll through your scene, and you begin to see and make contact with people, some familiar, some new, who see you in this calm state. As you greet and embrace one another, you realize that these are the same people who play a part in your real life, past, present, and future, and for the moment, at least, you are able to see them in radiant glory. This brings you a profound sense of joy.

After a time, you decide to lie down, and as you feel yourself drifting off into a light sleep, you begin to have dreams that are vivid in color, clarity, and meaning.... As your dreams continue, you find yourself able to step away and observe yourself having these dreams. This brings you contentment, and as you watch yourself and your dreams, you have a profound sense of who you are and how your life has meaning....

You take whatever time you want to dream all the dreams you want.... When you are finished, you arise, and this time, instead of walking, you begin running, slowly at first, then faster and faster.... You do not get tired, and instead you feel exhilarated.... Your body is moving fluidly and gracefully, and you can feel the wind rushing past you; the movement itself is intensely pleasurable.... You feel you could run like this forever, and though you decide to slow down and stop, just knowing that you could continue brings you a sense of unbounded strength and power.

After your run, you stop and look around and realize that you are now in a different place. Once again, both familiar and new, this place has a different feel. You are still calm and serene and actually energized from your run, and there is something alive about this new place. Everywhere you look, everyone you see, everything you touch is pulsing and breathing, even the ground upon which you are standing.... At first you aren't quite sure what to make of it, but after a few moments, the energy that is all around you seems endless and eternal. You feel yourself, your life force merging with those others around you, while at the same time maintaining your identity.... This exquisite feeling is once again, both familiar and new, and you remind yourself that you have had these feelings before....

You begin to walk again, feeling vibrant and more alive than you can remember.... The feelings are pleasurable, deep, and you feel welling up from inside you a laughter of the most magnificent sort. And as you continue walking, this laughter grows, filling every space inside you, until it comes pouring out, not just from your mouth, but from every fiber of your being…. It's a laughter for the ages, echoing from horizon to horizon…. While it may feel new to you, it is not unfamiliar. The laughter continues to pour forth for as long as you want, and when you are finished, you feel lighter and more elated than you can remember being ever before.

Ah, remembrance, you say. You decide to take a backward journey in time, and because this is obviously a magical time and place, you can easily do that. You begin your journey slowly, cautiously at first, and find yourself reliving, reexperiencing not only your personal past but also those of the people who were close to you during those parts of your life. You feel their feelings and know their thoughts…. For the first time, you experience true compassion for the imperfections, mistakes, and regrets that were and are a part of your past…. As you continue to travel back in time, the experiences accumulate, and though you are starting to feel overwhelmed by much sadness and loss for the way it might have been, you are also developing a profound sense of awe and reverence for your life and the lives of those who came before you.

You continue your backward journey, beyond your own life and on into the lives of your ancestors. As you pass through successive genera-tions, you see, hear, feel, taste, smell, and sense who you are and how you came to be you…. At first all the pieces don't fit, but the further back you go and the more you pay attention, the more solid you are beginning to feel…. Knowing yourself this way for the first time brings you feelings of tenderness and warmth that you never realized were a part of you. You stop your journey wherever appropriate and you can stay awhile just where you are….

When you are ready, you decide to come back to the original place and time just outside the theater…. As you do, however, something else occurs to you. *If I can go backward this way*, you say to yourself, *then I ought to be able to go forward as well*. As you ponder this notion, you realize that the moving forward is your life, that all of the feelings, thoughts, images, and sensations you have just experienced are parts of who you are, and that you want your future to include all of who you are….

114   You make a decision, a commitment, to a life filled and lived to its fullest. You know that moving forward can be lived only one moment at a time and you understand now, more clearly than ever, just what that means for you. You also realize that living this way won't necessarily make your life any easier, that the struggle is essential toward a life well lived, but you believe now that your life is yours to live in the most meaningful and purposeful fashion.... You are excited about this stance on your life, and as you get ready to return to the present, important messages will come to you.

Before you leave this realm, you turn back to gaze over the time and place you've just experienced.... As you reflect on what has just occurred and what you see, you feel a sense of wholeness, a sense that your life is perfect exactly as it is right now. Whatever happens from this moment on will be okay, and you are surprised to realize that you have known this to be true all along. And with that recognition and a smile on your face, you turn the page and begin reading part 3 of this book.

Toward a Balancing Future

Do not frivolously use the time that is yours to spend. Cherish it, that each day may bring new growth, insight, and awareness. Use this growth not selfishly, but rather in service of what may be, in the future tide of time. Never allow a day to pass that did not add to what was understood before. Let each day be a stone in the path of growth. Do not rest until what was intended has been done. But remember—go as slowly as necessary to sustain a steady pace; do on expend energy in waste. Finally, do not allow the illusory urgencies of the immediate to distract you from your vision of the eternal.

—Elisabeth Kubler-Ross
Death: The Final Stage of Growth

9

Facilitating Balance

T his chapter focuses on those people who help others achieve a sense of balance, whether in the workplace, with families, or with individuals. I talked with therapists and psychologists, career counselors, organization development professionals, and human resource specialists. Some of them work inside organizations with the explicit charter to help their companies become more productive. Others see clients who come to them asking any or all of the generative balancing questions. In either case, their role of facilitator is vitally important today, and each of them told me about the difficulties and struggles faced by their organizations and clients.

Though our interviews focused on how they work with others, many of these helpers are wrestling with balance in their own lives. The notion of "Healer, heal thyself" is well known to them, and they are very aware of the complexity of living in and teaching about balance at the same time. They impressed upon me, both in their stories and in their own lives, the idea that balancing is not a single, static place to be achieved and then forgotten. It is an ongoing and lifelong process of movement toward a sense of balance, regardless of current circumstances in our work, families, and personal lives.

Another strong message came out in these interviews, as it did in some of the earlier ones. There are no simple or universal formulas, and each organization, family, and individual must engage the process in their own best way. These helpers noted that many of those they work with wish for a set of rules, a road map that makes life simple, smooth, and pain-free. In fact, they added, much of their work with clients and organizations is helping them to unlearn rules and formulas that no longer serve them well, then teaching clients and organizations how to bring balancing, or their own conceptualizations of health and well-being, into their work, families, and personal lives.

Leah Wilson

Psychotherapist who works primarily with couples and families

Leah sees that her clients want balance in their lives, but that many struggle with living and working that way. She helps them find effective ways to cope with stress and also to recognize that their lack of balance is not due to some failure on their part. Here is what she told me:

"Many families these days are feeling vulnerable and badly about themselves. Our kids getting what they need is today the real hot potato, very scary, and almost too hot to handle. There is a crisis over caretaking in our culture, where lonely children are in jeopardy and consoling themselves with consumerism. We have been walking away from the connective tissue of family and there is nothing yet to replace it. The hub of the issue is gender and the changing roles of men and women, and I have to remind my clients that 'It is not your fault; it is your problem,' while helping them to understand that we are all going through a profound sociological phenomenon. I work with my clients to identify their dreams and to show them ways to collaborate and negotiate through effective communication.

"I believe that we all need to slow down and think of ourselves and each other as responsible for the entirety of our various roles, which includes expanded and redefined ones for both women and men.

"My clients and other families and couples need to work hard to reduce their guilt, both by redefining roles and responsibilities, but also through understanding the social context of that redefinition. Sort out what the children really need and be prepared for continuous negoti-ating. Balancing is not about new forms of perfection, but rather is about self-acceptance."

Leah spoke about many parts of generative balancing and she recognizes that it is a struggle finding meaning in a culture so devoted to creating success. To counteract this, she helps her clients redefine success and look anew at the roles and responsibilities in their lives. Leah emphasized the social context that affects our capacity to bring our lives into greater balance.

Sheryl Hinzel

Manager of career development programs for a large public utility

Sheryl and her staff serve a population of fifty thousand employees, helping them develop a sense of control and direction in their work and lives. Given the current business environment and the history in an organization that has heretofore taken care of its people, this is a huge challenge. Here is her story:

"As my organization downsizes, there is a growing expectation that people will have to do more with less, which puts them in conflict with family needs. Furthermore, employees struggle with just what the company wants from them, when, for example, it promotes balance but then does not really support it. My staff and the company's employee assistance department are seeing an increasing number of managers who are self-demoting themselves to lower-level positions because they are unable or unwilling to live with the expectation of being all things to all people.

"One of the challenges I face is that senior management does not understand the experience of balancing—or worse, in my mind, is that they may understand and not care, because the bottom line is so compelling. Also, regulatory issues and the presence of unions make balancing workplace effectiveness and employee well-being more dif-ficult to achieve. Plateauing and the lack of career opportunities have led to lower results in job fulfillment statistics, along with increased disability and stress claims.

120   "There are several things going on in my organization that help. My own area is offering new workshops, including career/life planning, that help employees understand their values and priorities. They learn to recognize that all their needs won't be met in the workplace and they can then decide on the trade-offs necessary to get those needs met. Employee assistance is offering brown bag luncheon workshops, including support for single parenting and others that have really helped employees. And our fitness centers have been positive for employees, not only for the release of stress, but for longer range health maintenance as well.

"I believe that my organization needs to be more flexible in understanding family needs and issues. Telecommuting should be more widely available, and there should be more off-shift work that would allow employees to work at times other than the traditional nine to five. This reduces the need for and costs of childcare. Working parents should be allowed to take time off, in small, hourly increments, in order to be more involved with their children. All companies should make employees take their vacations because the rest and relaxation, the time away, are antidotes for burnout.

"On the other hand, employees should be honest with bosses about what is important and what they're willing and not willing to do. Never be afraid or ashamed to *not* work long hours, because you've got a life…. Corporations will be in big trouble if they do not respond to these needs for balance. Balance is an ongoing process. Don't wait until the kids are grown. By then it's too late."

Sheryl has a big job helping thousands of employees in her organization, yet she is able to keep it in perspective. She is well aware that her organization's culture and mixed messages work against balance, and yet she and her staff are doing what they can to counteract much of that imbalance. She emphasizes that communicating and negotiating—connecting skills—are important for her clients.

Marty Bochelle

Psychotherapist who sees a large number of men in his private practice

Marty has built a life and career in which balance is a centerpiece. He tries to instill some of the same ideas in his work with clients and finds that creating success is much easier than finding meaning. He has found that often men find it very difficult to move toward the latter. Here are Marty's words:

"When working with clients, I help them explore what their needs for intimacy and support are and how they get meaning in their lives. For most of my clients, this is usually through work or some other activity. I also have them examine their sexual and physical needs, as well as their need for spirituality and fun. My work really revolves around the idea of trusting their own ability to take care of themselves and a recognition that change in any or all of these realms is difficult. Men in our society have such little emotional support and I try to provide a place where they can talk about their pain and find additional sources of support beyond their families.

"My advice and suggested changes are brief. First of all, because there is so much alienation in the workplace, there should be ways to validate this and then methods created to make meaningful connections at work. Retreats might be one way to make contact with one another. I'm an advocate for universal health care, respect for the environment, and equal rights for everyone. I also believe we need to learn how to be, not just to do, and we should honor our needs for friendship, support, and fun."

Marty's interview and work with clients focus on finding meaning and renewal. He knows that this is a struggle for his clients, and he endeavors to provide time and space where they can learn how to make them more a part of their lives. He recognizes that spirituality, fun, and sexuality, as well as the honoring of pain, are vital for the health and well-being of his clients.

Carmela Cassarra

Therapist who also does career development work for a large academic institution

Carmela sees balancing as a central issue for her and many of her clients and understands that therapy and career counseling go hand in hand. She is also aware of the social and political context in which her clients live and work; she sees that many of the barriers we all face are embedded in the culture itself. Here are her words:

"My clients have a hard time tearing themselves away from their work while living in a culture that says, 'You can't find time to do what it takes.' I often give my clients the simple assignment to take two breaks in the coming week, and when they do it, they often realize just how important it is.

"I spend a lot of time and energy dealing with 'Yes, but...' resistance from my clients. Self-assessment takes time, and even those who welcome change need time to process. I suggest that people develop closure rituals around the end of the workday, so that there is time and space to be and to give quiet time for reflecting. The idea that 'I should be able to do this on my own' needs to change to seeing one another as resources and sources of wisdom. In my groups, participants draw the name of another person and make support calls to them once a week. Our culture devalues hanging out with others, and my satisfaction as a helper derives from teaching people how to connect and learning how to trust and respect one another as resources.

"Too much energy in any one area is a sign of imbalance. Most people today deal with information or other people, and we rarely use our hands and body in our daily activities. We need to get back to physical activities that are not organized, noncompetitive, and spontaneous. Without honoring this physicality, we cannot get back to balance."

Carmela recognizes the importance of connecting, not only to other people as support and resources, but also to the earth itself. She was also one of the rare interviewees to mention the importance of ritual, especially in letting go and closing out our workdays and weeks.

Paul Hamann

Psychologist specializing in patients whose addictions have taken away their entire sense of balance

Paul has been working with addicted patients for a number of years and knows that many never come to grips with their addictions and therefore cannot move toward balance. Some of this difficulty, he concludes, is not in just his patients, but in a society that overvalues the external and material in people's lives. Here are Paul's words:

"If patients are to overcome their addiction, they have to bring their conscious and unconscious into alignment. Many of my patients are preoccupied with family-of-origin conflicts and get caught living in the past. Others are able to live in the here and now, but are unable to look at their history to assess its impact on their current situation. I conclude that working on the internal life precedes behavioral changes.

"Getting my patients to seriously work with their unconscious, I have to get them enthralled, interested, and appreciative, and eventually in control. Our culture's bias toward the conscious, rational, and linear makes my work all the more difficult, as I see real resistance and fear of delving into the unconscious. I am always working against the clock, and the fragile alliance I build with my patients could blow up at any time. My own balance thus comes less from changes I see in my patients and more from my own internal estimation of my work.

"The primary imbalance in our society is an overemphasis on consumption, which has a detrimental effect on all of us. Our belief that balance can be achieved through consumption rather than through one's internal homeostasis forces a dependency on external products. People have to then lead an addictive lifestyle to be filled and feel whole, and we come to believe we are inadequate without the product.

"There has got to be a change in our values, that we need to take a great gamble, by making radical changes in our economy and people's frames of reference. We need to begin living our values, and if we would create this kind of climate, that would be great."

For Paul and his patients, much of what works against finding balance is that we live in a society of creating success and consumption. He would like to see us move toward a culture of finding meaning and renewal, and this would make his work easier and more effective. Because his patients struggle so much with their addictions, Paul has recognized that rather than focusing on a cure or solution, he instead lets the work itself be his measure of the quality of his efforts.

Jane Walsh

Specialist in career management and outplacement

Jane sees that the changing economy and resulting changes in workplaces are making it difficult for her clients to achieve a sense of balance. She notes, however, that if organizations are to attract and retain needed employees, they will have to recognize that balance is important in the lives of many people. Jane shares her story:

"I think about the symbol of a juggler, balancing balls of equal weight. In reality, the balls are not the same weight or the same size. The majority of my clients are struggling with changing careers and lifestyles that enable them to work out a more satisfying life for themselves and their families. I see the 1990s as the 'We' generation where people are looking at balance as a primary goal. Organizations must look at this in order to attract and retain employees.

"Delayering has created huge stress, especially on mid-level managers whose duties have increased, while family pressures have not been reduced. I see a lot of insecurity in my clients, with people being afraid to complain, unwilling to take risks, and in some cases, almost paralyzed. Because of this insecurity, planning is difficult and people are feeling unsettled and continually frustrated by the limits they see. My answer is that we all need to build our own sense of internal security.

"More organizations are recognizing work and family issues, and a number of them have actually created positions to examine the needs in these areas. Some of the solutions include things like managerial coaching of employees regarding their careers, more tolerance for the needs of parents, and looking at the kinds of assignments that will give women more mobility into senior management. There is lots of talk regarding flexible hours and shared jobs, creating a 'mommy force' to mirror children's schools hours, but this usually turns out to be low-end jobs only.

"I would like to see recognition given to volunteerism and a strong focus on community involvement. This could be built into an organization's performance appraisal process, which would then recognize and reward the time commitment this takes. Organizations so often send mixed signals regarding their community involvement, seeing it as important for their image, but not being truly supportive of individual employee involvement.

"Young adults should explore very carefully lifestyle and career issues, rather that just falling into patterns of traditional roles. And for people of all ages, a key question for discussion should be, 'What kind of career gives both satisfaction and the lifestyle I want?' Groups of people inside organizations should come together in 'issues forums' to discuss the stresses and pressures they face every day. To ignore [these] is what really affects productivity and morale. In conclusion, we must look at the subject from a female perspective, because balancing for women revolves around the double day of work and childcare/home maintenance. We have so far to go regarding what's equitable.... We have to deal very significantly with what happens after work."

Jane recognizes that balancing is a crucial concern for organizations, not only as a retention issue, but also in terms of how it affects employee productivity. With all the changes going on in our workplaces, she is clear that our sense of security must come from the inside out; otherwise, we will always be at the mercy of outside forces. This is one of the main reasons generative balancing is important today. Furthermore, Jane believes that community involvement is important for all of us and that for health and well-being, taking time out and away from our usual routine is essential.

Pamela O'Ryan

Leisure consultant

Pamela works with people to help them understand the importance of leisure and then how to bring more of that into their lives. Here are her words:

"The balance between work and leisure is what makes for happier living, and the whole idea of life planning should include planning for leisure, as well as career. We shouldn't forget about love in any plans we make! In my workshops, I explain that leisure is time apart, time when you do not feel obligated to do something. I often ask my groups three questions: 'How many are pleased with the way your leisure is spent?' 'Would you know what to do with three free hours?' and 'How many have no leisure?' Invariably, many raise their hands in response to this last question.

"The changes I'd like to see begin with organizations. They should broaden their attitudes toward people and look for ways to help them through things like flexible schedules, alternative work schedules, job sharing, and so on. Individuals can do a time study for themselves, where they write down how they spend their time over a two-week period. After crossing out what they have to do, what is left is their leisure. Most people have more leisure than they think, and by amalgamating errands and tasks, there are ways to get larger pockets of time. People should cut out leisure activities that no longer make them happy.

"My words of advice are the following: First of all, look at what makes you happy, let go of what doesn't, and do more of what you want. Next, say no if you don't like something. Also, think about how you spend your off-work time as seriously as you do your work time. If you can't get satisfaction from one area, get it from the others. And look at the quality of your leisure, not the quantity. Finally, by giving intelligent thought to leisure, work, and family, you might find some way to improve your life without having to reach the point of burnout."

Pamela was one of the few interviewees who spoke explicitly about love, and the tone of our interview made it clear that she operates in this realm quite easily. Her emphasis on leisure is important in that she wants us to think about our off-work time as seriously as we do our work time. Pamela reminds us that flexibility, one of navigating's attitudes or beliefs, is as important for us as individuals as it is for our places of employment.

Meg Lee

President and owner of a human resources consulting firm

Meg's firm specializes in diversity training. She acknowledges that most companies do not fully appreciate the depth and subtleties associated with diversity and that we must recognize that valuing differences encompasses much more than the all-too-typical one-day training programs organizations now offer to their managers and employees.

"There are four areas of challenge in helping organizations to achieve a better balance. First of all is creating equity between employees who face the need for balance and those employees who do not. Secondly is helping organizations to understand the issues facing their employees who are juggling so many duties. Thirdly is helping organizations to understand the impact of stress on worker productivity. Stress is created as a result of the employee's inability to achieve balance. And fourth is helping organizations accept the need to create a work environment which values, respects, and celebrates diversity.

"There are several changes that would lead to a better balance between work and personal lives. First of all is accepting the fact that traditional ways of defining family do not apply anymore.... Dual-income families are a must in today's economy, not a luxury. Next, we need to accept the reality that more and more fathers are interested in finding ways to balance their personal and career lives in the same way that women are. Make your needs known by communicating what your issues are to those you work with. And, finally, network! Through networking, you can often identify important linkages to help."

Meg has identified several important ideas relating to generative balancing. First is the impact of stress on productivity. This influence, she says, is due to the lack of balance in people's lives. She also talks about the importance of awareness in diversity, just as the model says it is an aspect of renewal. Further, her closing words about networking, while given on the level of creating success, could just as easily be applied to connecting and finding meaning. Finally, she recognizes that men as well as women want and need balance in their lives.

Max Telizari

Career development consultant

Max works with organizations and individuals, and he sees that people are struggling, not just with balance, but sometimes just to stay employed. He suggests that balancing is important but, given our society's values, won't be easy to achieve. Here are Max's words:

"When I hear the word *balancing*, I think of integration. It's tough for people in organizations right now, because they are being pulled more by the organization and there is less time for balance. Because of fear and necessity, people are making compromises, sacrifices, and settling for less. Many people are glad just to have a job, earning money, and being gainfully employed. At the same time, many people are relocating into my area, there are fewer opportunities and those that exist are often lower-paying jobs. People are more restless and not as rooted in their communities, making it difficult to create meaningful contacts.

"I am noticing that people have more focus on family and are also looking for a sense of belonging. In my practice, I see lots of relocating employees who are nervous and apprehensive about finding a job and who are also wanting to feel connected to a community. I try to help my clients make some of these connections, and through my own strong network, I link them to professional and community organizations. This helps people not to feel so transient.

"Awareness is the first stage of achieving balance. Then we should do a thorough self-assessment of the various real and ideal aspects of our life, so that we realize where it is that changes are needed. Then we must commit to getting others who are close to us involved in the decisions. We should seek cooperation, assistance, help, and support, because when doing this alone we tend to fall back on old habits. I'm seeing that employers seem to me more humane and concerned about their employees than at any other time. There is more across-the-board compassion, concern, and goodwill."

Max recognizes that organizations are now more aware of many of the balancing issues he brings up here. Generative balancing posits renewal as the energy of balancing, and Max believes that the process begins with awareness and being conscious. Finally, Max is aware that our imbalance is causing us to act and react from a place of fear, that these "restless" times make it very difficult for us to achieve balance in our work and lives.

Claire Venturian

Director of training and organization development for a rapidly growing manufacturing firm

Claire believes that balancing is an important part of her organization's culture and recognizes that if balancing is not modeled by those in power and at the top of the organization, it will not be strongly supported or recognized as valuable. Her words are as follows:

"I recognize that many of our employees are in the midst of personal stress and professional ambition, complicated by parenting needs.

Many of these employees have explicit questions about the relationship between their home life and their effectiveness at work, and by the time they come to me for counseling or advice they are usually in a high stress mode. Many male employees are asking, 'Can I stay competitive [in my work and career] and maintain a sense of home life?' There are some good role models at the top of the organization, in particular an executive vice president who has young children. His saying 'I need to be home with my children' legitimizes home life. As a result, I see more people willing to take charge of their schedules.

"My organization experiences peak and valley times. During the peak times, which can last for months, there is less flexibility for employees and it becomes difficult to maintain balance. These times are particularly difficult for single parents, who do not have a partner to whom they can hand off some or all of the nonwork responsibilities. There is a genuine respect for balance in this organization and there is almost a bias against the workaholic.

"To make balancing easier for employees, it is important first that employees go to their managers with their needs and concerns. This allows employees to step down or move sideways without negative repercussions. This organization has a philosophy of developing managers for 'breadth and depth' and this gives employees more fluidity and more lateral movement than the traditional upward-only mode. This integration, as well as developing employees as members of a team, helps both the organization's succession needs and the employees' career plans. We also offer an employee assistance program for those employees whose stress is getting out of hand.

"If I were to advise the heads of other organizations, I would first want them to remember the struggles and stages they faced or still face in raising their own families and how that impacted their careers. This would help them to get some perspective and recognize that people bring their life to work. Remember, you are hiring the skills *and* the life they bring to the workplace. And we need to remember that when hiring new employees, all their transition stuff, including letting go of their previous situation, comes with them. The key question, of course, is 'How do we best get this person to be a contributing member of our organization?' "

130   In Claire's organization, balancing is being built into the culture, and various human resource practices are emerging to support it. This includes the flexibility in developing employees that meets both the organization's needs and the employees' needs as well. She added two things, not mentioned earlier, having to do with seeing people as whole, whether at work or elsewhere, and recognizing that people bring their "transition issues" with them whenever they enter a new situation.

Hermione Greene

Program director for a large nonprofit career center that provides services for both individuals and organizations

Hermione recognizes that balancing is increasingly important to her center's clients, acknowledging that it can be difficult because of workplace changes and a lack of connectedness that many experience in their relationships. Here is what she says:

"I am hearing the words *integration* and *alignment* a lot, with the question being, How do I integrate my time at work with who I am as a total person? Many of our clients are in their forties and fifties, and this being out of alignment is felt keenly by an increasing number of people who are less willing to put up with things that way.

"People feel isolated and often don't have others to talk to. There is a hunger for exploring these issues with others, but there is frustration at not having the time to devote to it. Furthermore is the ambiguity of it all—no charts, no maps...it is a very idiosyncratic search. I'm not sure how much workplaces will see this need, and I think an institutional response may not be the answer. I wonder why managers are not modeling flexible or alternative work arrangements.... We have to depend on ourselves and each other, because even the most responsible organizations cannot be responsive enough.

"Three issues conjure up the essence of balancing for me. First is value alignment. Second is a sense of community, which has to do with touching others and giving something back to them. Thirdly is the idea of self-renewal, which has to do with, if you can't move or have to stay [where you are] as the best or only realistic answer, how do you look at growth and what do you do to enrich and renew yourself?

"We need to be kind and patient with ourselves. Learning about who we are and what we value serves as a rudder that gives clarity and guidance in all areas of life. We have to learn not to expect too much from ourselves and to let go of our need for perfectionism. You can be a perfectly decent person by sitting still."

Hermione calls for patience, flexibility, and self-acceptance—letting go of a need for perfection. Whether the word is *alignment*, *integration*, *balancing*, or something else altogether, Hermione realizes that balance in our lives and work is made much easier if we remember our connections with others and cultivate them.

In helping their clients look inside and work toward balancing, all of these helpers recognize that this often creates conflicts, dilemmas, and the need for compromise and adaptation. Much of facilitation time and skill, then, revolves around helping clients to make the best decisions they can in balancing their values with the real world they live and work in at any given time.

And though less explicit, the necessity for remembrance is important not only for helping others, but also in many ways as a key to generative balancing. Through exploring the various aspects of our personal, ethnic, religious, spiritual, and family histories, we come to know who we are and what we want and need in the world. This brings with it feelings of wholeness and connection, often referred to as being grounded or centered, which in turn allow us to move into the future more assuredly and fluidly. Then we begin to see and know the real fruits of generative balancing.

Issues and Challenges for Facilitators

1. Your clients, if they internalize and follow your guidance, may find themselves moving into risky territory.

132

2. It is a challenge recognizing and understanding the social, political, economic, and cultural contexts that make balancing so difficult for clients.

3. It is a fine balance to hear the pain and suffering of clients and at the same time not take it in, thus avoiding one of the major sources of helper burnout.

4. It is sometimes easy to feel overwhelmed by how much there is to know and do in order to really help your clients.

5. It is hard to avoid a need to try to fix or solve a client's problem yourself.

6. It is a challenge teaching clients and organizations how to feel secure and have a sense of control in an age of uncertainty and continuous change.

7. It takes special skill recognizing and acknowledging power issues and struggles between men and women that are often subtle, hard to pinpoint, and tough to work through.

8. It is important to see clients as whole people rather than focusing only on the present problem or issue.

Strategies for Working Through the Issues and Challenges

1. Do the best you can to live by the words you give to your clients.

2. Work toward understanding and clarity of the various contexts your clients live and work in. This may require extensive and continuous study of issues not having direct application to your work.

3. Advocate to those in power for changes that will make balancing easier and that in the long run benefit everyone.

4. Teach your clients that balancing is an ongoing and lifelong process.

5. Let go of your own perfectionism. Do what you can and what is realistic. Learn to appreciate yourself and your work as it is, not as you believe it should be.

6. Focus on the process of your work with others and the outcomes and results will take care of themselves.

7. Create and enact rituals for yourself and clients, having to do with transitions, appreciation, grieving, and closure.

8. Take time out for self-renewal and gaining a sense of perspective on your work and life. An annual "renewal retreat" alone or with like-minded colleagues is an excellent way to bring balance into your life and to refresh yourself.

9. Most importantly, take care of yourself. Your work is vital to the health and well-being of all of us, and we need all of you to help show us the way in our own work and lives.

Moving Toward Grace
and Greatness

Generative balancing offers a guiding metaphor for thinking about and behaving in new ways that can guide us to lives and work of greater productivity, health, creativity, and happiness. It offers a way for us to reclaim our common sense and begin to look at the world differently. Generative balancing attempts to offer methods, techniques, and, I hope, the inspiration to begin building a future that is exciting, prosperous, safe, healthy, wise, and compassionate. As we move toward grace and greatness in this way, we will weave together in our work, family, and personal lives the will and capacity for creating success, finding meaning, and renewing ourselves.

Grace and greatness are the overarching results of being guided in our lives and work by generative balancing. *Grace* refers to the place or state in which we experience ourselves, others, the world, and the interactions among them as part of the divine. All our efforts, actions, feelings, thoughts, all of who and what we are, are couched in loving context, and when we notice it or experience it, we feel a sense of awe, beauty, and grandeur. It is this experience that is the core of all religions and is, I believe, the highest aspiration for all human beings.

Greatness is the physical embodiment and manifestation of this energy. Cathedrals, temples, monuments, and great works of art and music are examples of grace manifesting in greatness. I believe our energy and efforts are guided by our desire to achieve it, and thereby touch the divine in visible and tangible ways. That this idea often gets distorted at times in no way diminishes our want and need, our yearning to build greatness into our work and lives.

Just as the Chinese yin and yang symbol forms a whole, so, too, do grace and greatness. Many readers will recall that Freud and others spoke of love and work as the two great tasks of life; others have labeled this as intimacy and mastery, being and doing, sky and earth. Each of these symbolizes who we are and what we are becoming, and neither side is full or complete without the other. Our task, as we enter the twenty-first century, is to weave together grace and greatness to create a prosperous, meaningful, and fulfilling future for ourselves and subsequent generations.

Generative balancing is offered as a way intended to help us bring more of both sides of the continuum into our lives and work. As you read in the interview chapters and no doubt experienced in your own lives, it is during the times when moving in the direction of grace and greatness that we are at our best and most fully alive. If we could live, work, and relate to one another from an active mind-set of grace and greatness, just imagine how our lives and workplaces might be different.

Generative balancing reminds us that there are many ways to earn a living and can help us know how to make the necessary changes and find the pathways to do so. It can remind us that work is not only a way to make a living but is also a source of meaning and renewal in our life.

It can also help bring a fresh perspective to personal life: Though you may be just as pressed for time as before, you do not have to get caught in the same rush as everyone else. You will be more able to stay in your body, to feel your feelings, and to move through your day with focus and deliberation. You will begin to make time to be alone and enjoy the quiet, even if this is only for a few moments a day. You will wonder how you ever got through your days previously without this time for yourself.

Your relationships and interactions with others, from intimates to acquaintances and strangers, will also begin to change. Hopefully, you will find it easier to be honest and clear with others, while at the same time remaining sensitive to their feelings and need to be treated with respect and dignity. You may be more able to ask for what you need and want, and perhaps will even find yourself drawing different kinds of people toward you, and letting go of earlier relationships that may no longer work.

You should begin to feel lighter and more energized, able to laugh for more and different reasons. You may be able to play more, recognizing play as an end in itself. You may be just as competitive as ever, but you will realize more clearly the nature of the game and will begin to loosen the grip on having to win or having to always be or do better.

You will probably find yourself in the process of becoming a different person, one who in many ways will look unchanged to the casual observer. But you will feel the difference in subtle ways. With generative balancing completely in place, people can more readily see both sides of the story and see at least some truth in nearly everyone's point of view, recognizing that all the disparate pieces and personalities make up not a cacophony, but an elegant tapestry, one that we can perhaps even make some sense of. When this starts happening, people will respond to you differently and will think of you as a leader and a wise person—except that you will have a distinct sense that this does not make you anything special or deserving of privileges that others can't or don't have.

As you begin to change, so, too, will those who come in contact with you. As you begin to internalize and practice generative balancing in your work and life, you will be an example of living and working according to your own emerging sense of balance, and in that way will inspire others to move toward their own sense of grace and greatness.

As individuals and families move toward grace and greatness, the impact on organizations will be felt more strongly, and they will begin to respond. Some of these changes are already well under way. As more of us live by generative balancing, our organizations will be forced to change, and generative balancing will begin to permeate workplace culture. And slowly, as people, policies, and culture are influenced in small, imperceptible ways, our organizations will be transformed.

What will our workplaces begin to look like? Some common characteristics will probably emerge. They will be more fluid and flexible, both in product and service and how they operate internally. Employees will have more options about when and where they work, and will not have to continually justify why they need to do this. These organizations' planning processes, human resource practices, infrastructure, and even the culture itself will hold flexibility and adaptability as keys to a viable future.

This flexibility will not come easily or without costs. There will be resistance to change, just as there is now, and some of the players will simply no longer fit. Organizations will restructure periodically, but instead of being driven only by cost concerns as they are today, they will instead begin to think about the long-range consequences, determining whether and how a more effective organization is emerging. Many employees and leaders will have to be trained how to think in these new ways, and how to act with generative balancing always in mind.

A balancing organization will be more democratic and egalitarian. Job titles will be less of an issue as pay and rewards go to those who demonstrate competence. This will also help break down barriers that women and minority cultures continue to face each day. Lateral job movement, broadening experiences, and training that teaches people how to see and understand the whole picture will be more the rule than the exception. Decision making will be spread out and down into the organization, with all members having access to the information necessary to make informed choices. Some organizations may go so far as to elect their leaders and managers, and when those do not perform to expectations, they then can be voted out.

Furthermore, increased participation will lead the balancing organization into shared ownership, which in turn becomes the basis for shared governance. Whether this is in the form of employee stock ownership programs or something as yet undreamed of, a balancing

organization will recognize that shared ownership is the best way to
create a sense of common purpose and is the only chance of keeping the
loyalty of its employees. The balancing organization can expect that its
employees will make an investment in their ownership. It won't and
shouldn't be a gift or entitlement. This sharing will extend also to those
who work part-time, those who are temporary, and those who are
contractors or consultants. The balancing organization will understand
and support involvement from all its players.

There will be greater trust throughout the organization, which is
fostered by leaders who sincerely and succinctly can say "I made a
mistake," "I don't know," and "I'm sorry." When cultures can live with
these admissions, trust will grow, and all members will feel freer to be
themselves. This in turn allows for more interaction among different
individuals, functions, and departments, while adding to the understanding all members will begin to develop about the entire enterprise.
When the newest member of the organization, as well as those with the
least status or power, think about the challenges facing the organization
in the same language as does the chief executive officer, then a
balancing organization has begun to emerge.

Balancing organizations will be active participants in their communities, supporting and even guiding local, national, and global initiatives. Whether it is child or elder care and other needed and
noncontroversial issues or even political, social, or cultural causes that
are provocative, a balancing organization will not shy away from these
larger responsibilities and will not be afraid to take a stand for what it
believes in, even at the risk of losing some business. It will realize that
in the long term, doing what is right is what really matters.

Finally, and perhaps most importantly, a balancing organization will
continually question everything about what it does, including those
basic assumptions upon which it exists. It will ask such hard questions
as "Must we continue to grow this way? If so, what are the long-range
costs and benefits of such a strategy? What are the alternatives to a
growth strategy?" and "Is the customer always right? If we are always
reacting to customer demands, are we necessarily doing the right

thing?" and "Is profit always our main goal and reason for being? If so, are there ways to build profit formulas that consider the needs for balance and the long term? If not, what is our goal and reason for being, and how do we build an organization to support them?" Whether a balancing organization changes as a result of these and other questions is less important than that it be willing to confront these questions.

As individuals, families, and organizations move toward grace and greatness, what other results are we likely to see? I believe we will see ourselves growing in ways that until now have eluded us. We will be more aware of each other's needs and will have more tolerance and patience for one another. Strong communities and the desire to belong to them will become a norm, with schools and schooling as the highest priorities in those communities. As we begin to learn and live with generative balancing, we will be more capable of dealing with any adversity we might face, because we will have greater depth and breadth of resources from which to draw. And we can expect that we will let go of much of our death-denying attitudes and behaviors, freeing us to grow old gracefully and to value and honor our elders.

Organizations will see the quality of everything they do improve. They may be at a loss as to how to measure some aspects of this or to say exactly what is behind the changes, but everyone in those organizations will feel the differences. There will be better and more timely responses to all stakeholders, whether their interest be in customer service, employee relations, or community building. There will most certainly be higher productivity, even though, paradoxically, less energy will be focused on direct production processes and numbers. Because employees will care about what they are doing there, and because the organization is seriously committed to a quality workplace, employees will much more freely give who they are in support of the organization's mission. Productivity, however it will then be measured, most certainly will grow.

How do I know that any of this will come to pass as I've described it? I don't! But if you look around at all the hopeful signs and new ideas that are bubbling up around us, you might draw some of the same conclusions I have. It is my hope that enough of you agree and are at some point willing to participate in what I see as the potential for a wondrous unfolding in our work, family, and personal lives.

Strategies for Creating Success

- Strive to find and do work that you are passionate about.
- Take the risks you believe will help you achieve your goals. Learn from them all, especially those that do not turn out so well.
- Document regularly and in detail your goals and the steps to their achievement.
- Keep yourself current and up-to-date by reading, talking with others, and formal and informal study.
- Recognize that being "good enough" as, for example, a parent, worker, or lover really is good enough.
- Learn that there is much in life beyond your control, and let go of your need to control it.
- At least once a year ask yourself, What does success mean to me? Share your answers with significant others.
- Develop your imagination through daydreaming, visualization, drawing, painting, music, wandering, and any other ways to free up your mind.
- At least once a year, do a thorough assessment and reflection of the previous year and be sure to document what you learn.

Strategies for Finding Meaning

- At least once a day, ask yourself, Who am I?
- Make time in your day or week to hang out with others, even if it means your tasks get done at a later date.
- Involve yourself in a cause or idea that moves you deeply.
- Turn off your television now and then. Turn it on only when there is something worth watching.
- In any encounter you have with another human being, make a real effort to listen to that person.

142

- Give yourself permission to feel all your feelings and do not ever apologize for crying.
- Recognize and work toward being comfortable with the fact that you will die someday.
- Open yourself to meeting and interacting with others who are different than you. Meet them on their terms at least half the time and allow yourself to be changed by having met them.
- Draw a picture, write a poem, call an invocation, or in some other way describe the meaning or purpose of your life and work. Keep these symbols close to you and ponder them frequently.

Strategies for Renewal

- Make time regularly for quiet and solitude.
- Find a spiritual practice that resonates deeply within you.
- Keep sources of inspiration such as words, music, or pictures close to you and make them a part of your life.
- Make physical activity a regular part of your daily routine.
- Regularly ponder the future and its unlimited possibilities.
- When you find yourself wrestling with paradox, don't struggle to resolve it. Let paradox just be a part of how you live and work.
- Bring love into every aspect of your life and work, and begin communicating your love to others.
- Create and enact rituals of transition that mark and honor significant events in your life and work.
- Bring awareness of the future of the next generation and the planet itself into your everyday routine. Let this awareness influence your life and work.

Before closing this chapter, I want to share some philosophical musings that represent the basic assumptions of generative balancing and how to live well in the turbulence of modern times.

1. *Act as if the future of the planet depended on how you act here and now.* Develop a sense of responsibility for all your actions, however small

or inconsequential. Pay attention to your behaviors and be prepared to own up to their consequences.

2. *Slow down in all aspects of your life*. Though this may sound ludicrous to busy and successful people, this is one of the keys to having the focus and energy to do what you want and be who you are. This also creates space for intimacy, seeing things as they are, and catching glimpses of the divine.

3. *Be willing to sacrifice now and then for others and your community*. Realize that the world does not revolve around you and your needs and that ultimately it is healthier to give than to receive. This may entail suffering and force you to confront evil. We are stewards of the earth and beacons for the future.

4. *Be conscious of your choices and learn to discern your needs from your wants*. We must recognize that many of our choices, priorities, and desires are socially conditioned and are not truly needs. As we learn this discernment, our vision and purpose will become clearer.

5. *Begin each day by remembering where you came from and who you are*. Remembrance is essential in moving toward grace, and it is a big part of greatness as well.

6. *Let go of the desire to be right or perfect*. These victories say little or nothing about the kind of person you are or are becoming.

7. *Recognize that the process itself is the essence of life*. Wherever you start from, however far you get in this life, the only true reality is right here and right now. Life is an unfolding, a journey, not a problem to be solved.

8. *Connect physically with others and your surroundings*. Hold and touch others. Allow them to hold and touch you. Rest when you are tired. Spend time touching and being touched by the earth.

9. *Let your dreams and imagination be your guide into the future*. By allowing these to guide you, you can create a direct link between your deepest wisdom and all possible futures.

10. *Involve yourself with children, whether you have any of your own or not*. Children are our direct link to the future and they need our strength and wisdom.

11. *Don't ever stop questioning*. The philosopher Abraham Joshua Heschel said, "In knowing how to ask the right question lies the

144

only hope of arriving at an answer."[8] The poet Rainer Maria Rilke said, "Be patient with all that is unsolved in your heart. Try to love the questions themselves like locked rooms and like books that are written in a foreign tongue.... Live the questions raw."[9] Continuous questioning is the wellspring of lifelong learning and the essence of generative balancing.

As a way to conclude this chapter, I want to engage two of my heroes in an imaginary dialogue that captures in a very few words what moving toward grace and greatness and generative balancing is meant to be. The participants are Henry David Thoreau and Mary Catherine Bateson, with me as the facilitator.

MG: Henry David, will you share with us what you have learned?

HD: I learned this, at least by my experiment: that if one advances confidently in the direction of his dreams, and endeavors to live the life which he has imagined, he will meet with a success unexpected in common hours.[10]

MG: Go on.

HD: If you have built castles in the air, your work need not be lost; that is where they should be. Now put foundations under them.[11]

MG: Mary Catherine, I'd be interested in your response.

MC: Composing a life involves a continual reimagining of the future and reinterpretation of the past to give meaning to the present, remembering best those events that prefigured what followed, forgetting those that proved to have no meaning within the narrative.[12]

MG: Anything to add?

MC: Composing a life through memory as well as through day-to-day choices, that seems to me the most essential to creative living.[13]

MG: Yes, creative living! Henry David, what is your take on this idea?

HD: We must learn to reawaken and keep ourselves awake, not by mechanical aids, but by an infinite expectation of the dawn, which does not forsake us in our soundest sleep. I know of no more encouraging fact that the unquestionable ability of man to elevate his life by conscious endeavor.... To affect the quality of the day, that is the highest of arts.[14]

MG: Mary Catherine, anything you'd like to add?

MC: Each of us had to search in ambiguity for her own kind of integrity, learning to adapt and improvise in a culture which we could only partly be at home.[15]

HD: Why should we be in such desperate haste to succeed in such desperate adventures? If a man does not keep pace with his companions, perhaps it is because he hears a different drummer. Let him step to the music he hears, however measured or far away.[16]

MG: Mary Catherine?

MC: Individual improvisations can sometimes be shared as models of possibility for men and women in the future.... In finding a personal path among the discontinuities and moral ambiguities they face, they are performing a creative synthesis with a value that goes beyond the merely personal.[17]

MG: Can you expand on this?

MC: We must live in a wider space and longer stretch of time. In thinking about survival, we must think of sustaining life across generations. The need to sustain human growth should be a matter of concern for the entire society, even more fundamental than the problem of sustaining productivity.[18]

HD: When we are unhurried and wise, we perceive that only great and worthy things have any permanence and absolute existence, that petty fears and petty pleasures are but the shadow of reality. This is always exhilarating and sublime.[19]

MG: Any other thoughts from either of you?

HD: All nature is your congratulation, and you have cause momentarily to bless yourself. The greatest gains and values are farthest from being appreciated. We easily come to doubt if they exist. We soon forget them. They are the highest reality. Perhaps the facts most astounding and most real are never communicated by man to man. The truth of my daily life is somewhat intangible and indescribable as the tints of

146 morning or evening. It is a little star-dust caught, a segment of the rainbow which I have clutched.[20]

MC: We must celebrate the mysterious sacredness of that which is still to be born.[21]

MG: Thank you both so much!

Acknowledgments

There are a number of people without whose love, support, and guidance this book would have remained only a dream. First, my wife, Carol, is a tremendous grounding force for me, and her planful, levelheaded way keeps my natural idealism in the real world.

Sara, my daughter, is rapidly becoming a young woman as this book is being written. She and I spend a lot of time together, all of which is important to me. She is a great inspiration.

Dora, my mother, is the most loving and accepting person I've ever known; her unwavering belief in me remains a major source of motivation.

My brothers, Bruce, Larry, and Neil, are an integral part of my past and future. Their presence is with me always, and in many ways, the words here are owed to them.

I have had a number of inspiring, compassionate teachers over the years, and I'd like to thank them for their wisdom and support. Many colleagues and friends have shared my enthusiasm for this project and have made suggestions and given feedback that has improved the book in ways too numerous to mention. Thanks also to the thousands of students, clients, and workshop participants who have continually taught me to listen, to stretch, to not assume too much, and to keep asking the hard questions.

148   Much thanks also goes to Consulting Psychologists Press. Lee Langhammer Law has been a continuing source of energy and enthusiasm, and her feedback and guidance have made it possible for this book to come about amidst a good deal of humor and grace.

Most of all, I want to thank the people who were interviewed for the book, those many people who opened their lives and hearts to be a part of this. Their wisdom, kindness, and grace under pressure kept me in awe throughout the writing. My deepest appreciation to each one of you.

Appendix:
The Interview Process

As I designed the interview process for this book, it was my intention to collect, record, and report stories from a variety of people from various walks of life who live and work in different parts of the United States. I feel confident that, had the same interview questions been posed to another group of seventy-plus interviewees, the responses would have revealed information similar to what you have read in the interview chapters of this book.

My interviewees were selected based simply on whether they had some notion of and sensibility for the concept of balancing and were willing to talk about that with me. I began with people I knew—friends, acquaintances, and colleagues—and then asked them to refer me to people in their circles who might speak to me about balancing. After the first twenty-five interviews, most of which were conducted with Californians, I began to specify location, age, gender, and ethnic origin requirements in order to have my total sample better reflect the larger American society.

As I expected, not everyone I contacted wanted to be interviewed. Some were not interested and many of the others were too busy. Still others were suspicious of my motives or, among those who didn't know who I was, thought I was trying to sell them something.

Most of the people I contacted, though, were eager to talk. I interviewed people in one of three ways: face-to-face, over the telephone, or through a written questionnaire. In all cases, the questions remained basically the same, except that with the written interviews I was not able to probe or ask for further details. The face-to-face interviews were the most intimate and enjoyable—I met with people at their offices, in their homes and mine, at coffeeshops and restaurants, anywhere where we could comfortably talk. I made a point to talk with couples and families in their homes, and sometimes, children were present. I spoke to managers for the most part in their offices in order to get a feel for the organizational energy they were referring to when they spoke of their workplaces. I spoke with helpers and facilitators in their offices so I could get a sense of the environment in which they counseled. The interviews were scheduled to last forty-five minutes, but most were at least an hour. The ones conducted in the home tended to be the longest, averaging seventy-five minutes and sometimes lasting as long as two hours.

The telephone interviews, which are about 50 percent of the total, also were scheduled to last for forty-five minutes. They ranged from thirty minutes in one case to as long as ninety minutes. The average length, as with the face-to-face interviews, was about one hour. With virtually all of the phone interviews, I had never met the interviewee, nor had I ever seen him or her. These interviews continually surprised me with their openness, intimacy, and people's readiness to tell me stories and anecdotes that were important to them.

The written interviews, about 10 percent of the total, were the least satisfying and, on the whole, the least revealing. The questions may have been too open-ended, and the context was not well enough established to really draw people out. Some of the briefer stories and quotes in the text come from these interviews.

I recorded most of the face-to-face interviews and all of the telephone interviews on paper, taking notes as fast as I could. I tape-recorded some of the couples and families I met with, mainly because it was otherwise difficult to keep track of two or more people's remarks, especially when more than one person was talking at the same time. After the interviews, I transcribed the notes and recordings into a several-page narrative of what I had just heard. I tried to be accurate and faithful to what I heard in the interviews, and in some cases had to add a few words to smooth the narrative. I apologize for any possible misquotations or misinterpretations.

I made a decision early in the interview process to do a "light" identification of my interviewees. Rather than presenting a lot of detailed information about age, ethnic origin, work, and family situation, I felt the subject of balancing would be better served by letting the interviewees' own words speak for themselves. I gave all interviewees the option to change their names for publication, but only a few did so. However, understandably, I have changed their names to protect privacy. Most who worked in large organizations asked that their organizational affiliation not be identified or at least be disguised.

I worked with eight basic questions in all the interviews, but changed the emphasis, and even the context, depending on one of four points of view I asked my interviewees to take. Those four points of view were as an individual, as a couple/family, as an organization member, and as facilitator/helper. Obviously, a large number of the interviewees fell into more than one group, and often the interviews spilled over into other areas. Regardless of the point of view, my questions were usually asked in the same order, and sometimes were combined. Also, many of the interviewees were so eager and interested in the subject that after the opening question they did not need additional questions to keep the interview going. The questions were:

1. When you hear the phrase "Balancing work, family, and personal life," what comes to your mind?
2. What are the issues/challenges you face daily, short-term, and longer-range in balancing your work, family, and personal life?

3. What does balancing look and feel like for you?
4. How close are you to balancing, and what gets in your way of moving toward that?
5. What are you doing to bring balance into your work, family, and personal life?
6. What changes in organizations, society, family, etc., would help you in moving toward balancing? Be specific, please.
7. What advice and words of wisdom do you have for others in balancing work, family, and personal life?
8. Anything else on the subject of balancing you consider important and worth sharing?

As far as the demographics, my original intention was that the interviewees would be a microcosm of American society. As it turned out, and as can be seen in the demographic data shown in table 1, most of the interviewees are professionals, managers, and entrepreneurs, are well educated, and have fairly high incomes. I think a further study of other segments of our society would prove interesting and worthwhile. Every one of the seventy-plus people I interviewed was asked to fill out a demographics sheet (see figure 5), but as you can see in the questionnaire, I gave people the option to not respond to any questions with which they were uncomfortable, an option some exercised. Also, in the bottom section, a number of interviewees checked more than one category, especially in the area of their work affiliation. Fifteen interviewees, all of whom live in states other than California, did not return questionnaires. Their data would not have greatly altered those reported in figure 5. (All percentages are rounded to the nearest whole number; therefore, not all totals will equal 100 percent.)

I hope that as you read the book you picked up just how strongly people feel about this subject and just how important balancing is in their lives.

Demographic Questionnaire for Balancing Interview   153

The information below is anonymous and confidential. If any of the questions are objectionable, do not answer them.

Age: ❑ 20s   ❑ 30s   ❑ 40s   ❑ 50s   ❑ 60s   ❑ 70s

Sex: ❑ Female   ❑ Male

*Ethnic origin:*_____

*Religion:*_____

Highest formal education:
❑ High school   ❑ AA   ❑ BA/BS   ❑ MA/MS/MBA, etc.   ❑ Ph.D./M.D., etc.

*Job title:*_____

*Industry:*_____

Number of people who work in your organization:
❑ 1–25   ❑ 26–100   ❑ 101–500
❑ 501–1,000   ❑ 1,000–3,000   ❑ 3,000+

Annual salary:
❑ Under $20,000   ❑ $20–$35,000   ❑ $35–$50,000
❑ $50–$65,000   ❑ $65–$80,000   ❑ $80,000+

Hours per week at work:
(Include time preparing for, commuting to and from, and time on the job, etc.)
❑ Less than 20   ❑ 21–30   ❑ 31–40   ❑ 41–50   ❑ 51–60   ❑ 61+

Current residence: City_____   State_____

Check the most appropriate role:
    ❑ Manager/Decision maker in an organization
    ❑ Employee in an organization
    ❑ Helper/Change agent
    ❑ Other (please describe):_____

Status:
    ❑ Single, no children
    ❑ Single, children
    ❑ Married, no children
    ❑ Married, children
    ❑ Step/Blended family
    ❑ Live with significant other, opposite sex
    ❑ Live with significant other, same sex
    ❑ Other (please describe):_____

Figure 5   Balancing Questionnaire/Interview Demographic Data

154   Table 1   Demographic Data Compiled From Balancing Interviews

Age		Sex		Ethnic origin	
30s:	36%	Female:	69%	Asian:	6%
40s:	52%	Male:	31%	Black:	6%
50s:	7%			Latino:	4%
60s:	2%			White:	84%
70s:	4%				

Religion

Armenian: 2%	Baptist: 2%	Catholic: 17%
Episcopalian: 7%	Jewish: 21%	Lutheran: 2%
New Age/Metaphysical: 9%	Presbyterian: 2%	Protestant: 5%
Unitarian: 13%	Not applicable or declined to state: 20%	

Highest formal education		*Annual salary*
High school:	6%	Less than $20,000: 4%
Associate degree:	2%	$20,000–$35,000: 8%
Bachelor's degree:	26%	$35,001–$50,000: 33%
Master's degree:	55%	$50,001–$65,000: 19%
Doctorate degree:	11%	$65,001–$80,000: 13%
		Over $80,000: 23%

Job titles

Area Manager; Associate Director; Attorney; Career Counselor/Consultant; Consultant; Dean; Director; Director, Client Services; Director, Management and Organizational Development; Director, Marketing; Employee Relations Manager; Guidance Counselor; Human Resources Manager; Manager; Marketing Manager; Marketing Services Administrator; Owner; Personnel Analyst; President; Project Planner; School Psychologist; Senior Administrative Assisstant; Senior Analyst; Senior Vice President; Technical Support Specialist; Therapist; Vice President; Vice President, Administration.

Industries

Banking; Biotechnology; City Government; Computers; Consulting; Data Processing; Digital Imaging; Education; Fashion; Financial Services; Funeral Services; Human Services; Insurance; Nonprofit; Paper Manufacturing; Retail; Transportation; Utility; Zoo.

Table 1   Demographic Data Compiled From Balancing Interviews (continued)

Number of people
who work in your organization   *Hours per week at work*

1–25	20%	Less than 20	2%
26–100	15%	21–30	11%
101–500	25%	31–40	15%
501–1,000	3%	41–50	38%
1,000–3,000	12%	51–60	24%
Over 3,000	25%	Over 60	11%

Current residence

Arizona: 2%	California: 65%	Florida: 6%	Illinois: 2%
Louisiana: 2%	Maryland: 2%	Minnesota: 2%	Missouri: 2%
Nevada: 2%	North Carolina: 4%	Oregon: 2%	Texas: 2%
Washington: 2%	Wisconsin: 2%		

Role   *Status*

Manager/decision maker:	55%	Single, no children:	10%
Employee:	13%	Single, children:	14%
Helper/Change agent:	32%	Married, no children:	12%
		Married, children:	38%
		Step/Blended family:	5%
		Significant other, opposite sex:	10%
		Significant other, same sex:	10%

Notes

Introduction

1. A. de Tocqueville, *Democracy in America* (New York: Anchor Books, 1966), 703.
2. A. Zajonc, "Contemplating Nature," *Noetic Sciences Review 23* (Winter 1992), 20.

Chapter One

3. K. W. Kelley, ed., *The Home Planet* (Reading, MA: Addison-Wesley, 1988), 42.

Chapter Four

4. I. Progoff, *At a Journal Workshop* (New York: Dialogue House Library, 1975), 47.
5. M. Cardinal, *The Words to Say It: An Autobiographical Novel*, translated by Pat Goodheart (Cambridge, MA: Van Vactor and Goodyear, 1983), 69.
6. M. S. Peck, *The Road Less Traveled* (New York: Touchstone, 1978), 131.

Chapter Eight

7. IBM Corporation, "Balancing Act" Advertisement, 1992.

Chapter Ten

8. A. J. Heschel, *Man Is Not Alone: A Philosophy of Religion* (New York: Farrar, Straus & Giroux, 1951), 43.
9. R. M. Rilke, *Letters to a Young Poet*, translated by Stephen Mitchell (New York: Random House, 1986), 34.

158 10.   J. W. Krutch, ed., *Walden and Other Writings by Henry David Thoreau* (New York: Bantam Books, 1962), 343.
11.   Krutch, 343.
12.   M. C. Bateson, *Composing a Life* (New York: Penguin, 1989), 30.
13.   Bateson, 34.
14.   Krutch, 172.
15.   Bateson, 13.
16.   Krutch, 345.
17.   Bateson, 232.
18.   Bateson, 234.
19.   Krutch, 176.
20.   Krutch, 265.
21.   Bateson, 240.

Selected Bibliography

F or sake of brevity, I have cited only one source from each author, or if coauthored, there may be a second listing. The reader who is so inclined will find that many of these authors have numerous other writings that are worth reading.

Ackoff, R. L. *Creating the Corporate Future*. New York: Wiley, 1981.

Adams, J., ed. *Transforming Work*. Alexandria, VA: Miles River Press, 1984.

Albrecht, K. *The Creative Corporation*. Homewood, IL: Dow Jones-Irwin, 1987.

Anderson, S. R., and Hopkins, P. *The Feminine Face of God*. New York: Bantam Books, 1991.

Angelou, M. *I Know Why the Caged Bird Sings*. New York: Random House, 1970.

Barry, K. *Susan B. Anthony: A Biography of a Singular Feminist*. New York: New York University Press, 1988.

Bateson, M. C. *Composing a Life*. New York: Penguin, 1989.

Baxter, G., and Baxter, N. K. "Einstein's Advice on Work in the Next Century." *Personnel Journal* (April 1986): 14–19.

Beach, B. *Integrating Work and Family Life: The Home-Working Family*. New York: State University of New York Press, 1989.

Beckhard, R., and Harris, R. T. *Organizational Transitions: Managing Complex Change*. Reading, MA: Addison-Wesley, 1977.

Bellah, R. N., Madsen, R., Sullivan, W. M., Swindler, A., and Tipton, S. A. *Habits of the Heart: Individualism and Commitment in American Life*. New York: Harper & Row, 1985.

Berman, M. *The Reenchantment of the World*. Ithaca, NY: Cornell University Press, 1981.

Block, P. *The Empowered Manager: Positive Political Skills at Work*. San Francisco: Jossey-Bass, 1987.

Bolen, J. S. *Gods in Everyman: A New Psychology of Men's Lives and Loves*. San Francisco: Harper & Row, 1989.

159

160
Bolles, R. N. *The Three Boxes of Life*. Berkeley, CA: Ten Speed Press, 1978.

Bridges, W. *Transitions: Making Sense of Life's Changes*. Reading, MA: Addison-Wesley, 1980.

Bruner, J. S. *The Process of Education*. Cambridge, MA: Harvard University Press, 1963.

Bureau of National Affairs. *Work & Family: A Changing Dynamic*. Washington, DC: Bureau of National Affairs, 1986.

Byrne, E. F. *Work, Inc*. Philadelphia: Temple University Press, 1990.

Capra, F. *The Turning Point: Science, Society and the Rising Culture*. New York: Bantam Books, 1982.

Cardinal, M. *The Words to Say It: An Autobiographical Novel*, translated by Pat Goodheart. Cambridge, MA: Van Vactor and Goodyear, 1983.

Cleveland, H. *The Knowledge Executive*. New York: Truman Tally Books, 1985.

Coates, J. F., Jarratt, J., and Mahaffie, J. B. *Future Work: Seven Critical Forces Reshaping Work and the Work Force in North America*. San Francisco: Jossey-Bass, 1990.

Conrad, D. R. *Education for Transformation*. Palm Springs, CA: ETC Publications, 1976.

Csikszentmihalyi, M. *Flow: The Psychology of Optimal Experience*. New York: Harper & Row, 1990.

Davis, S. M. *Future Perfect*. Reading, MA: Addison-Wesley, 1987.

Deutschman, A. "Pioneers of New Balance." *Fortune*, 20 May 1991, 60–68.

Drucker, P. F. "The Coming of the New Organization." *Harvard Business Review* (January–February 1988): 45–53.

Dyer, L. "Bringing Human Resources into the Strategy Formulation Process." *Human Resource Management* 22 (1983): 257–271.

Eckenrode, J., and Gore, S., eds. *Stress Between Work and Family*. New York: Plenum, 1990.

Edmondson, B. "Remaking a Living." *Utne Reader* (July–August 1991): 313.

Elgin, D. *Voluntary Simplicity*. New York: Bantam Books, 1981.

Fassel, D. *Working Ourselves to Death*. San Francisco: Harper San Francisco, 1990.

Finkelstein, J., and Newman, D. A. H. "The Third Industrial Revolution: A Special Challenge to Managers." *Organizational Dynamics* 13 (1984): 53–65.

Fombrun, C., Tichy, N., and Devanna, M. A. *Strategic Human Resource Management*. New York: Wiley, 1984.

Frankl, V. E. *Man's Search for Meaning*. New York: Pocket Books, 1959.

Gardner, J. *Self-Renewal: The Individual and the Innovative Society*. New York: Norton, 1981.

Gibb, J. *Trust: A New View of Personal and Organizational Development*. Los Angeles: Guild of Tutors Press, 1978.

Gilligan, C. *In a Different Voice*. Cambridge, MA: Harvard University Press, 1982.

Golden, K., and Ramaniyam, V. "Between a Dream and a Nightmare: On the Integration of the Human Resource Management and Strategic Business Planning Process." *Human Resource Management* 24 (1985): 429–452.

Googins, B. K. *Work/Family Conflicts: Private Lives—Public Responses*. New York: Auburn House, 1991.

Gould, R. *Transformation: Growth and Change in Adult Life*. New York: Simon & Schuster, 1978.

Griffin, D. R., ed. *Spirituality and Society: Postmodern Visions*. Albany, NY: SUNY Press, 1988.

Grudin, R. *The Grace of Great Things: Creativity and Innovation*. New York: Ticknor and Fields, 1990.

Grunwald, H. "The Year 2000: Is it the End—Or Just the Beginning?" *Time*, 30 March 1992, 73–76.

Handy, C. *The Age of Unreason*. Boston: Harvard Business School Press, 1989.

Harman, W. *Global Mind Change. The Promise of the Last Years of the Twentieth Century.* Indianapolis: Knowledge Systems, 1988.

Harris, P. *Management in Transition*. San Francisco: Jossey-Bass, 1985.

Heller, J. *Catch-22*. New York: Dell, 1961.

Heschel, A. J. *Man Is Not Alone: A Philosophy of Religion*. New York: Farrar, Straus & Giroux, 1951.

Hirschhorn, L. *The Workplace Within: Psychodynamics of Organizational Life*. Cambridge, MA: MIT Press, 1988.

Hochschild, A. *The Second Shift: Working Parents and the Revolution at Home*. New York: Viking, 1989.

Hutchins, R. M. *The Learning Society*. New York: Praeger, 1968.

James, W. *The Varieties of Religious Experience*. New York: Collier Books, 1961.

Johnson, R. *Ecstasy: Understanding the Psychology of Joy*. San Francisco: Harper & Row, 1987.

Johnston, C. M. *The Creative Imperative*. Berkeley, CA: Celestial Arts, 1984.

Kanter, R. M. *When Giants Learn to Dance*. New York: Simon & Schuster, 1989.

Karasek, R., and Theorell, T. *Healthy Work: Stress, Productivity, and the Reconstruction of Working Life*. New York: Basic Books, 1990.

Keeney, B. P. "What is an Epistemology of Family Therapy?" *Family Process* 21 (1982): 153–168.

Kelley, K. W., ed. *The Home Planet*. Reading, MA: Addison-Wesley, 1988.

Kidder, R. M. *An Agenda for the 21st Century*. Cambridge, MA: MIT Press, 1987.

Kiechel, W., III. "The Organization That Learns." *Fortune*, 12 March 1990, 133–136.

Kinberly, J. R., and Miles, R. *The Organizational Life Cycle*. San Francisco: Jossey-Bass, 1980.

Kimberly, J. R., and Quinn, R. E. *New Futures: The Challenge of Managing Corporate Transitions*. Homewood, IL: Dow-Jones-Irwin, 1984.

Koestenbaum, P. *The Heart of Business*. San Francisco: Saybrook, 1987.

Koller, A. *The Stations of Solitude*. New York: Morrow, 1990.

Kohn, A. *No Contest: The Case Against Competition*. Boston: Houghton Mifflin, 1986.

Krutch, J. W., ed. *Walden and Other Writings by Henry David Thoreau*. New York: Bantam Books, 1962.

Kubler-Ross, E. *On Death and Dying*. New York: Macmillan, 1968.

Kummerow, J. M., ed. *New Directions in Career Planning and the Workplace*. Palo Alto: Consulting Psychologists Press, 1991.

Labich, K. "Can Your Career Hurt Your Kids?" *Fortune*, 20 May 1991, 38–56.

Lee, C. "Balancing Work and Family." *Training* (September 1991): 23–28.

Leonard, G. *Mastery: The Keys to Long-term Success and Fulfillment*. New York: NAL-Dutton, 1991.

Lippitt, G. L. *Organizational Renewal*. Englewood Cliffs, NJ: Prentice-Hall, 1969.

Ludeman, K. *The Work Ethic: How to Profit From the Changing Values of the New Work Force*. New York: Dutton, 1989.

Lunneborg, P. W. *Women Changing Work*. New York: Greenwood Press, 1990.

Lynd, R. S., and Lynd, H. M. *Middletown: A Study in American Culture*. New York: Harcourt Brace Jovanovich, 1929.

Maslow, A. H. *The Farther Reaches of Human Nature*. New York: Viking, 1971.

May, R. *The Courage to Create*. New York: Bantam Books, 1975.

McDargh, E. *How to Work for a Living and Still Be Free to Live*. Reston, VA: Reston, 1985.

Miles, R., and Snow, C. "Designing Human Resources Systems." *Organizational Dynamics* 13 (1984): 36–52.

Miller, D. M., ed. *The Lewis Mumford Reader*. New York: Pantheon, 1986.

162   Miller, D., and Kets de Vries, M. *The Neurotic Organization*. San Francisco: Jossey-Bass, 1984.

Millman, D. *The Warrior Athlete*. Walpole, NH: Stillpoint, 1979.

Mills, D. Q. *The New Competitors*. New York: Wiley, 1985.

Mintzberg, H. "The Effective Organization: Forces and Forms." *Sloan Management Review* 32 (1991): 54–67.

Misa, K., and Stein, T. "Strategic HRM and the Bottom Line." *Personnel Administrator* (October 1983): 27–30.

Mitroff, I. *Business Not As Usual*. San Francisco: Jossey-Bass, 1987.

Morgan, G. *Riding the Waves of Change*. San Francisco: Jossey-Bass, 1988.

Mumford, L. *The Transformations of Man*. New York: Harper and Brothers, 1956.

Nadler, D. "Managing Transitions to Uncertain Future States." *Organizational Dynamics* 11 (1982): 37–45.

Naisbitt, J., and Aburdene, P. *Re-Inventing the Corporation*. New York: Warner Books, 1985.

Neill, A. S. *Summerhill*. New York: Hart, 1960.

Osherson, S. D. *Holding On or Letting Go: Men and Career Change at Mid-Life*. New York: Free Press, 1980.

O'Toole, J. *Vanguard Management: Redesigning the Corporate Future*. Garden City, NY: Doubleday, 1985.

Owen, H. *Spirit: Transformation and Development in Organizations*. Potomac, MD: Abbott, 1987.

Pearce, J. C. *The Crack in the Cosmic Egg*. London: Lyrebird Press, 1973.

Peck, M. S. *The Road Less Traveled*. New York: Touchstone, 1978.

Postman, N., and Weingartner, C. *Teaching as a Subversive Activity*. New York: Delta, 1969.

Progoff, I. *At a Journal Workshop*. New York: Dialogue House Library, 1975.

Quinn, R. E., and Cameron, K. S., eds. *Paradox and Transformation: Toward a Theory of Change in Organization and Management*. Cambridge, MA: Ballinger, 1988.

Rilke, R. M. *Letters to a Young Poet*, translated by Stephen Mitchell. New York: Random House, 1986.

Robertson, J. *Future Work: Jobs, Self-Employment and Leisure After the Industrial Age*. New York: Universe Books, 1985.

Rogers, C. *On Becoming a Person*. Boston: Houghton Mifflin, 1961.

Rohrlich, J. *Work and Love: The Crucial Balance*. New York: Summit, 1980.

Rubin, L. B. *Intimate Strangers: Men and Women Together*. New York: Harper Colophon Books, 1983.

Salska, A. *Walt Whitman and Emily Dickinson: Poetry of Central Consciousness*. Philadelphia: University of Pennsylvania Press, 1985.

Saltzman, A. *Downshifting: Reinventing Success on a Slower Track*. New York: Harper-Collins, 1991.

Schaef, A. W. *When Society Becomes an Addict*. San Francisco: Harper & Row, 1987.

Schmookler, A. B. *Out of Weakness: Healing the Wounds That Drive Us to War*. New York: Banton Books, 1988.

Schneider, J. "The Transformative Power of Grief." *Noetic Sciences Review* (Autumn 1989): 26–31.

Schumacher, E. F. *Small Is Beautiful: Economics as if People Mattered*. New York: Harper & Row, 1973.

Sekaran, U. *Dual-Career Families*. San Francisco: Jossey-Bass, 1986.

Senge. P. *The Fifth Discipline*. New York: Doubleday, 1991.

Sher, B. *Wishcraft: How to Get What You Really Want*. New York: Ballantine, 1979.

Silverstein, S. *The Giving Tree*. New York: Harper & Row, 1964.

Simonton, O. C., Matthews-Simonton, S., and Creighton, J. L. *Getting Well Again*. New York: Bantam, 1978.

Skolnick, A. *Embattled Paradise: The American Family in an Age of Uncertainty*. New York: Basic Books, 1991.

Slater, P. *The Pursuit of Loneliness*. Boston: Beacon Press, 1976.

Smelser, N., and Erickson, E. *Themes of Work and Love in Adulthood*. Boston: Harvard University Press, 1980.

Sorokin, P. *The Crisis of Our Age*. New York: Dutton, 1943.

Stata, R. "Organizational Learning—The Key to Management Innovation." *Sloan Management Review* 30 (1989): 63–74.

Tannenbaum, R., Margulies, N., and Massirik, F. *Human Systems Development*. San Francisco: Jossey-Bass, 1985.

Tart, C. T. *Waking Up: Overcoming the Obstacles to Human Potential*. Boston: New Science Library, 1986.

Theobald, R. *The Rapids of Change*. Indianapolis: Knowledge Systems, 1987.

Tichy, N., and Devanna, M. A. *The Transformational Leader*. New York: Wiley, 1986.

Tillich, P. *The Courage to Be*. New York: Yale University Press, 1952.

Tocqueville, A. de. *Democracy in America*. Garden City, NY: Anchor Books, 1966.

Toffler, A. *Powershift*. New York: Bantam Books, 1990.

Tulku, T. *Gesture of Balance*. Oakland, CA: Dharma Publishing, 1977.

U. S. Congress, Office of Technology Assessment. *Technology and the American Economic Transition: Choices for the Future*. Washington, DC: U.S. Government Printing Office, 1988.

Vaill, P. B. *Managing as a Performing Art: New Ideas for a World of Chaotic Change*. San Francisco: Jossey-Bass, 1989.

Viscott, D. *Risking*. New York: Pocket Books, 1977.

Wachtel, P. L. *The Poverty of Affluence: A Psychological Portrait of the American Way of Life*. New York: Free Press, 1983.

Watts, A. W. *The Meaning of Happiness*. New York: Harper & Row, 1940.

Weisbord, M. *Productive Workplaces*. San Francisco: Jossey-Bass, 1987.

Welwood, J., ed. *Challenge of the Heart: Love, Sex, and Intimacy in Changing Times*. Boston: Shambala, 1985.

Williams, T. A. *Learning to Manage Our Futures*. New York: Wiley, 1982.

Zajonc, A. "Contemplating Nature." *Noetic Sciences Review*, 23 (Winter 1992), 17–21.

Zuboff, S. *In the Age of the Smart Machine: The Future of Work and Power*. New York: Basic Books, 1988.

Index